COOL HOMES
IN HOT PLACES

COOL HOMES IN HOT PLACES

Suzanne Trocmé

Photography by Andrew Wood

COLLINS DESIGN

An Imprint of HarperCollins*Publishers*

HarperCollins books may be
purchased for educational,
business, or sales promotional
use. For information, please
write: Special Markets
Department, HarperCollins
Publishers Inc., 10 East 53rd
Street, New York, NY 10022.

First published in 2006 by:
Collins Design,
An Imprint of
HarperCollins*Publishers*
10 East 53rd Street
New York, NY 10022
Tel: (212) 207-7000
Fax: (212) 207-7654
collinsdesign@harpercollins.com
www.harpercollins.com

Distributed throughout the
United States by:
HarperCollins*Publishers*
10 East 53rd Street
New York, NY 10022
Fax: (212) 207-7654

Publisher: Jacqui Small
Editorial Manager: Kate John
Designer: Lawrence Morton
Editor: Catherine Rubinstein
Production: Peter Colley

Library of Congress Number:
2006928007

ISBN-10: 0-06-089038-X
ISBN-13: 978-0-06-089038-4

Printed in Singapore

First Printing, 2006

contents

controlling
the environment

Global warming is coming to us all, despite ongoing debate as to the details of its impact. Add to that the fact that increasing numbers of temperate-dwellers are adopting warm-climate second homes as an escape from modern life, and it becomes essential to adapt to hot living, to do so sustainably and with style.

In a hot land, the aim is both to minimize the impact of the heat and to take advantage of its benefits: to even out its extremes and take shelter from the worst of it, at the same time as using its energy to best effect in terms of power consumption. Throughout the whole process of creating a home, from initial choice of terrain, through selection of specific site and orientation, to choice of materials and even details such as color, heat is a prime consideration. The challenge can be met through lo-tech and largely passive means—age-old methods of building or ventilating—as much as through modern and interventionist techniques; and along with stemming rising temperatures, it is important not to overlook the value of creating an ambience of cool calm even when the actuality is otherwise.

There is no such thing, however, as an ultimate sustainable or environmentally friendly building system. Each project, each site, each building must be approached on an individual basis: in other words, a holistic approach that looks at all the factors that impact on a site, the occupants, its region, climate, culture, and resources, before a strategy is employed. The site will have its own microclimate, affected by surrounding terrain, buildings, elevation, vegetation, and so on. Knowing all these factors can help a designer orientate a building to take advantage of them, turning it to catch the sun or wind, or shifting it a few degrees so that tall trees provide shade. According to a build's surroundings and the owner's priorities, choices will be made, for instance to avoid or gain sun.

Aspect not only concerns views, therefore, but an entire quagmire of devices required to set up orientation of a home so it functions successfully both against and with the elements. The aim is to control the environment.

Orientation is the first consideration, since it determines where you build your home and in which direction it faces. Designer Andrzej Zarzycki spent five days with his clients driving around their South African game farm near the Botswana border before deciding where exactly the house should be built (see pages 30–3). They chose the perfect spot: the principal house, a labyrinth of lodges, stands on a hillside overlooking the most exquisite plain for game watching—and directly at the favorite watering hole of local baboon; they also have a penchant for game watching, so now the swimming pool has become the first port of call for the baboon, who frequently join the owners for breakfast! Not so much a mistake as a wise and instinctive decision, which possibly indicates that we are closer to nature than we might imagine when it comes to house-building!

The most obvious way to keep a home cool is to prevent it from heating up too much in the first place. In any terrain, simple design strategies can be employed to minimize heat gain from the sun by having adequate shelter from it. Siting a structure in the shade of a hillside or trees, sinking it deep into the ground, or building it with thick walls and insulating materials (such as local stone) can all be effective techniques for keeping cool, and basic siting can be amended with details such as overhanging eaves or foliage. As Frank Lloyd Wright put it, "The physician can bury his mistakes, but the architect can only advise his client to plant vines."

Size and positioning of windows is also fundamental. Very few of the houses covered in this book have windows of similar size all the way around the perimeter walls. While in temperate climes we may crave sun, in hot homes we are mainly trying to keep it out, or at least control it. Sometimes large picture windows are used only on the side of the house where there is the least direct sun—preferably along with the best view, or the waterside if there is water—with tiny windows, mere slits, in the sunniest wall, in order to keep out the fierce summer light and heat. In the environs of dusty Marrakech, however, we found the home of architect Karim El Achak (see pages 54–9) positioned to have large southerly windows so that the sun is present in the wintertime, and for the view of the Atlas Mountains. South-facing in California or the Mediterranean, for instance, may be too hot, but where the summer sun is directly overhead, nearer the equator, as El Achak points out, it does not enter the house at all. In such cases it may actually be late-afternoon sun from the west that provides the most solar heat gain. The point is there is no single correct approach; it is important to weigh up all factors and choose your priorities.

Sunlight is of course our friend as well as our enemy—we just have to know when to say "no" and shut it out or live in penumbra. In some cases, we may choose to use solar power to drive heating and even cooling systems, either by passive means such as solar windows (see page 135) or by more active methods, most typically solar panels (although they can be expensive), and this, too, will affect siting of windows.

Windows are also fundamental to ventilation, especially essential in humid heat. Air conditioning is not the obvious answer it may seem, since it generates greenhouse gases; systems with the highest emissions are beginning to be restricted by building regulations in the US and the EU, and are likely to be further constrained in the future. Our natural cooling systems are water and air, and there are many ways to use them. Aside from positioning openings so that they encourage through drafts, some deceptively simple cooling systems have evolved over time, and there is much to be learned from indigenous or vernacular architecture, a valuable basis for "green" design, in the tropics and in other parts of the world.

The traditional Malay house and the Ibans' longhouses of Southeast Asia are good examples. Both are wooden structures set on posts, with steep roofs and high ceilings, designs that mean good ventilation and cooling of interior spaces. Being up on stilts allows ventilation beneath the buildings, keeps living spaces above the flood line and limits the possibility of invasion

aspect is key to siting a hot home; a minor adjustment to orientation can make a huge difference.
RIGHT, TOP The concrete back of the property in Plettenberg Bay in South Africa (see pages 70–3): note the lack of windows on this north-facing, i.e. sunny, side. The house is orientated toward the beach, and the upper section is pivoted over the lower to take maximum advantage of the view.
RIGHT, BOTTOM To build on a hill looking out to sea may mean waiting for the right piece of real estate to become available. There is no second best. The Na Xemena house in Ibiza (see pages 86–91) has an unprecedented view, and the hills and water allow natural cooling of the interior and exterior spaces. There is in fact a property just below, which is not overlooked due to clever orientation.

1

2

3

4

5

6

7

8

9

by predators. The materials tend to be lightweight and therefore do not retain heat. Recently these traditional designs have been reinterpreted in more contemporary designs that utilize passive energy strategies.

In the Middle East, the ancient cooling towers known as *badgir* in Persian are still found in Iran, and are still cool inside when it is 100°F (38°C) outside. The simplest towers are rectangular, containing shafts with two to four shelves: the upper shelves catch incoming hot air and redirect it out again, while the lower ones recirculate cool air from inside. Air is cooled further by passing over a pool of water. The region's traditional skills with engineering are also evident in irrigation systems based on natural underground water channels; found from Morocco to Central Asia, they are called *karez* in the Xinjiang region of western China and *qanats* in Persia, where they originated. With skills like these, it is not surprising that by the 13th century the Islamic garden, for all its arid location from the Alhambra in Spain to the Taj Mahal in India, was such a stunning success. Water featured heavily, as did canopies of fruit trees that restricted re-radiation losses from the ground, trapping cool air that could be circulated through the house—another form of natural cooling.

Water can be a friend to cool any home by way of a pool, a water feature, or a vista of sea or lake. Although I firmly believe that a pool is useless if you live in, say, New England, it is a necessity in a warm climate, should water not be entirely scarce. Not only does it refresh all through the day—a quick dip is all it takes—but the mere presence of water is a tonic. A lake can bring a breeze, gentle or otherwise, and the ocean brings zest of life (and negative ions to boot) and the most delightful sounds, too. Water heats up much more slowly than air, so it remains cooler when the surrounding air is hot. It enables vegetation to grow, which in turn gives us shade and, together with the water, increases rates of evaporation. This is part of the reason that rural areas are cooler than urban ones: heat is lost in evaporation from streams and rivers and transpiration from trees (another reason is that concrete retains heat). Water can also be used to store heat.

light draws people, as it does flowers, but our need for light must be balanced with keeping cool. **LEFT, 1** In Marrakech small windows help keep the light out. **2** In dark shade in Johannesburg, a dining table comes to life with light streaming from deep ceiling recesses. **3** In Ibiza, a shaft of light is directed by a ceiling skylight in a double-height room; although bright, it is gentle. **4** Old and new architecture can coexist without apology, light bringing both to life. In Provence the light dances through a basket arbor. **5** "There are frequently links between the ecology of a building ... and the poetic dimensions of architecture—such as the fleeting effect of shadow patterns.... Perhaps one should define them under the heading of 'lifting the spirits,'" says Sir Norman Foster. Seth Stein in South Africa creates extraordinary pattern, with echoes of arbors. **6** Tall slit windows throw light onto an interior wall in North Africa for reflected light; the room remains cool. **7** White reflects light and helps spread it evenly. **8** Light, air, and sunshine were the new ideals in the Neues Bauen movement of the 1920s. Thirty years later, glass buildings became a reality, with air conditioning to regulate internal climate. **9** The rear of this house, a series of *fincas*, has small windows; its opposite side has window walls facing out to sea. **RIGHT** Nature, when manipulated, can find the best solutions to harsh sunlight, and vines and creepers will meld a home into its environment.

Building or adapting a home in a humid environment differs vastly from building in an arid one. Water can become the enemy when rot sets in if incorrect materials have been used. Local and indigenous ones are always best, built by nature to cope—look for hardwoods such as teak (a tip for updating a bathroom in any climate) and porous stone (so as not to slip).

A seminal building that truly represents well-thought-out orientation, not just for the choice of waterside position but also its structure, which takes advantage of such a position, thus the vision of the building itself, is the Sydney Opera House. Following a competition in 1956, the project was built by the Danish Jorn Utzon between 1957 and 1973. Utzon said in 2004, "In the construction process, we study the sources of human wellbeing more than anyone else.... The partner is thus in the broad sense *the place*. On land it's about a site and some surroundings—it may be a forest or a plain, with the wind conditions and the light that the place happens to offer, but at all events it's a partner that you have to relate to."

Two other successful waterside buildings that appeal to me enormously are Frank Gehry's titanium-tiled Guggenheim Museum in Bilbao, built in the city's docklands, and the earlier Malaparte house built by Groupe 7 on the Italian island of Capri. Like the Opera House, Bilbao is a gateway building, and Gehry struggled with its scale. It is a museum, I know, and huge, and self-confessedly metaphorical, but it feels completely human—a successful, "living" waterside development which, despite its dizzying undulating form, enhances the environment as well as protecting from it.

Casa Malaparte, built for writer Curzio Malaparte in the late 1930s, is a very friendly house on a steep cliff over water and was the first to incorporate the picture window—a picture-frame window where the view becomes the art. It does not follow any of the island's building manners, does nothing to camouflage itself, but nevertheless you cannot imagine any other place where it could have been built. Strong and marked lines, bulks added one upon another in a modular way, emphasize the rationalist origin of the architectural concept the building is based upon. A blueprint for modern waterside living, Malaparte used to be open to the public, but now has a tenant—so as much as I urge you to visit both Bilbao and Sydney, I am afraid Malaparte will have to elude you, apart from in books.

These three examples all make use of platforms or levels. Aspect involves volume and cannot be thought of in a rectilinear manner. Platforms are used to pull people through buildings, whether public or private, and create fluidity. As air has to circulate, so do people to make the best of a hot home. In Ibiza and North Africa we came across houses built as *enfilades* of boxes, either linked by a common hallway or built in the manner of Versailles, one box flowing from another over changing levels. In the south of France the house height had to be contained by local building restrictions, so the plan shows a leisurely incline upward using subtle platforms. In other schemes, spaces were hollowed out to provide escape from the elements. Spatial continuity minimizes the sense of enclosure.

air & water
are our natural cooling systems.
BELOW Water takes longer to change temperature, either upward or downward, than land does, so water is cooler than land by day and warmer at night. Air temperature is influenced by the land or water beneath it, and this difference in temperature, and consequently pressure, results in breezes: from water to land by day and from land to water by night. This is Merimbula on Australia's Sapphire Coast: architect Clinton Murray likes louvers, which assist air flow.
OPPOSITE Vertical air circulation occurs when air heats up. Its molecules spread out, and it becomes less dense than surrounding unheated air; it therefore rises, transferring its heat to a cooler region and allowing cool air to take its place—this is heat transfer by convection. Fans, seen here in a double-height room (good for convection) in Provence by Andrzej Zarzycki, also encourage air flow.

For nomadic populations space is rarely a problem, but water is imperative. The Rendille, for example, are African nomadic pastoralists whose movements are dictated by the need for forage and water for their camels—they live in the desert between the Ndoto mountains of Kenya and Lake Turkana. On finding water, Rendille women construct their home, a *min*, which has been carried in kit form by camel. This bent-pole and stick framework with sisal panels forms a kind of shell shape: two-thirds of a hemisphere with an inclined front, not unlike the some of our super-sized family tents. At the rear, a couple of animal hides are hung for shade, although they can be removed if the interior becomes too stifling. On plan, the *min* departs from the circle, being wider at the front than the rear. It is a delightful architectural shape. Although it quivers (it is lightweight, for transportation) in the fierce winds that come off Lake Turkana, this waterside structure is nevertheless sturdy and successful as shelter against heat and dust as well as wind. So sensitive are the Rendille to the environment, they take care not to overgraze land or pollute water. We should take heed on many counts. The structure not only behaves well in the elements, but is positioned directionally and aerodynamic in form. Despite ranting daylight temperatures in such regions, it is the lake that produces the most problematic condition: the wind. It seems ironic that the Rendille spend their lives seeking water, yet water becomes their enemy.

I believe that building cannot be looked at in isolation, and the core of this book explores living in a hot climate by terrain. Whether we aspire to hot-house living or have it coming to us through global warming, it is better to be prepared and see how the professionals do it, to look to the world.

terrain

Even in ancient times, humans understood the need for effective shelter and, on a lighter note, enjoyed a bit of a view. Whether now we choose to live waterside, hillside, or in the open prairie should still depend less on whim, if we are conscientious builders, and more on the potential effect of the elements and our response to them—although the notion of "aspect" can include our basic instinct for beauty: the view.

The climatic variables that affect human comfort are not only temperature (which depends on heat radiated from the sun and from our surroundings) but also humidity (water-vapour content of the air; in its most tangible form it becomes rain) and wind. Whether we feel too hot, too cold, or "just right" depends on the combination of these factors. Of course the fundamental influence over them is latitude—the nearer the equator we are, the closer and more directly overhead is the sun, and the higher the temperature—but conditions are also affected by altitude, topography, and winds.

In other words, the details of a site's position and its surrounding terrain have quite an impact on its climatic character. A hilltop, for instance, will be cooler than the local norm—temperature decreases with altitude (hence snow on mountain-tops even in hot regions)—as well as being more exposed to chill winds. Against these cooling influences, it will also be more exposed to the sun, unless cleverly tucked into the shade of an outcrop. Waterside locations, similarly, are cooler than inland, partly because water itself smoothes out extremes of temperature and partly because its differential heating triggers local breezes that have a cooling effect. Wooded terrain, meanwhile, offsets cool shade with warm humidity. And whatever the topography and vegetation, an urban area will suffer from heat more than its rural equivalent, due to the thermal mass provided by the built environment.

Different terrains therefore demand different approaches to building, both in terms of challenges posed and ways of tackling them. Architects will orientate their designs differently according to the priorities imposed by the position of the sun in the sky; the desired emphasis on cooling, power supply, or light; the shade offered by trees or topography; local winds; and of course views. In inhabited areas, they must also bow to planning regulations, but at least basic amenities will already be to hand. In terms of materials, the most readily available, aesthetically pleasing, and durable in each warm environment will be greatly influenced by whether the terrain is arid or humid, urban or wild. In all these respects, each terrain has its own ways.

wilderness

"Touch the earth lightly," runs an Aboriginal proverb, often quoted by one of Australia's finest architects, Glenn Murcutt, who grew up in Morobe, New Guinea. Touching the earth at all has become a rare and strange pastime for most of us in the so-called civilized world, with the hustle and bustle of cosmopolitan life. The closest some of us experience, sadly, will be Battersea or Central Park. Yet more and more people are wanting to "touch the earth" in daily life: increasing numbers—and I admire them—are choosing wilderness for their very own slice of the great outdoors, in a way that no longer means opting out as did Georgia O'Keefe (to Santa Fe) or D.H. Lawrence (for whom Yorkshire proved to be not wild enough).

It takes courage to live in the wilderness, in both emotional and practical terms. People who choose this option tend to be those who have arrived, who have lived successful lives and feel it's time for something different—in effect, the escapists.

It also takes time and planning, dedication and commitment. Building a habitable home in the wilderness, as opposed to a refuge for camping-style vacations, requires massive consideration and organization to provide utilities and essentials in an area with no infrastructure of cables, pipes, and communications—we are not just talking about home comforts but the very basics of life. It can be relentless if the temperatures are extreme and roads not even sound enough for transportation. Bringing in water and electricity is tough, and solar alternatives not always appropriate, since they may be expensive and not ideally attuned to local conditions.

On an aesthetic level, building in the middle of nowhere has enormous advantages. There is complete freedom of design, unconstrained on the whole by planning restrictions, and an open choice as to orientation and view: the imagination can run riot. People who build in these circumstances tend to want to use local, sympathetic materials, but leave their own stamp on the design, by bringing in an element from a neighboring region or by making a cutting-edge architectural statement, even though there is seldom anyone around to witness it.

Designs also reflect the fact that wilderness areas in warmer climes tend to be desert or semi-desert, so many of the challenges are about providing plentiful water and keeping cool. Roof terraces are crucial for desert homes, the coolest place to sit in the evenings, and subterranean rooms can play a valuable role. Although such homes have plenty of space to spread out across, quite often they are two or three storys high in order to gain the advantages of airflow and the panoramic views that come with height. Traditional wilderness dwellings, however, could be only single-story.

Building in the wilderness also requires consideration as to materials used: what will offer the best protection against extremes of heat (not only the burning sun, but also intense cold at night, as lack of cloud cover, trees, or water means daytime heat is rapidly lost)? What will best withstand winds bearing erosive grains of sand? It often means using adobe—sun-dried bricks, usually made from mud and straw—but not exclusively. The houses that follow are newly built in different wildernesses, one in North Africa, one in South Africa, and one in Arizona. One has its roots in adobe, another uses other traditional methods, and the third uses a combination of modern construction materials. All are breathtaking and all at one with their own, very specific, natures.

OPPOSITE A serene bedroom in a neutral color palette at the rear of the Arizona house built by architect Bart Voorsanger. Incised into the hillside, the house incorporates the wild landscape into its design.

Arizona dreaming
Eminent American architect Bart Voorsanger sees architecture as seeking and reinterpreting the sensuality inherent in nature, a "special, tactile and auditive experience." Soaring cantilevered metal reverse-curved pavilion roofs may sound incongruous for a wild Arizona canyonside, but the effect here is practically organic.

Nature comes and goes in architecture, stylistically speaking. But urban architects such as Manhattan-based, Princeton-and-Harvard-educated Voorsanger welcome the chance to attempt to capture nature in projects that allow freedom to build in wide open space. Voorsanger's passion for nature began following a trip to the Sierra Nevada with "mountain climbers, conservationists, photographers and devotees of the wilderness," including photographer Ansel Adams, no less. Voorsanger later became a mountain climber himself, but soon realized how dangerous nature can be: "When it is not

LEFT The angles of the French limestone fireplace in the living room accentuate the slant of the mahogany-clad ceiling in its rise from 9 to 18ft (2.7 to 5.5m). The house has a feeling of airiness—it is in fact air-conditioned.

RIGHT To witness the vertical ascent to the north there are 19ft-high (6m) glazed walls offering fantastic vistas.

FAR LEFT On approach, the building's exterior is stucco and stone. In the build, the landscape on the side elevations was disturbed to a width of only 4ft (1.2m).

LEFT Located in the high desert, just outside Tucson, abutting the Coronado Natural Forest, the property loses itself in the surrounding scrubby, stony wilderness with remarkable lightness of touch.

OPPOSITE The structure has two storys. The upper level contains the primary spaces, for living, dining, study, as well as the principal bedroom suite, situated on graduated platforms, each with a separate protective roof (see below).

LEFT Interior designer Eve Robinson became involved early in the project, sourcing furniture and furnishings. In the family room the geometric lines of the cabinetry are echoed in the grid-patterned backs of the René Gabriel chairs (c.1946). Knoll Bertoia barstools add a contemporary touch to the kitchen area.

BELOW Much of the interior was created from mahogany—the floors and ceilings throughout—sourced from tree farms.

respected, tragedies occur. Yet, simultaneously, nature's own fragility renders it vulnerable to suffering man's interventions."

With this in mind, we visit the high desert, one of the most fragile and least forgiving of all natural environments, at the northern edge of Tucson, Arizona, abutting the Coronado Natural Forest. This Coronado Ridge residence extends over 6,700 sq ft (620sq m) on a 3-acre (1.2ha) property, and yields spectacular views over the upper canyons. The placing of the house required a precise incision into the landscape, and to minimize disruption to the site and conserve energy, bedrooms and services were embedded on the lower level of the stepped site. The upper level contains the primary spaces, for living, dining, and study, as well as the principal bedroom suite, each situated on a graduated platform with a separate protective roof—to protect from the heat, that is. The three-tiered stepped roofs therefore cascade down the mountainside, giving deep overhanging projections; upward curves reveal the natural beauty of the canyon landscape above.

At once blending with nature and standing majestic in its presence, the building's exterior is stucco and stone. To the north are 19ft-high (6m) glass walls offering fantastic vistas of the vertical ascent, likewise to the south toward Tucson. The clients, Susan Daniels and Gene Frank, were determined

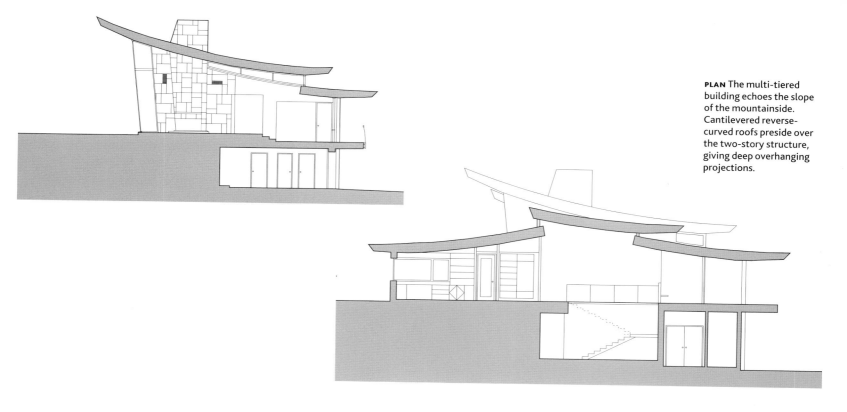

not to consider a standard *faux* adobe house—the kind that pepper the desert landscape in some areas.

What I find remarkable about this house is not only that it integrates so seamlessly into its landscape, built with nature in the forefront of the mind, but that it was designed for a couple who were relocating fulltime. A vacation home requires one way of thinking; a permanent home is quite a different animal. True to American standards, there is air conditioning, admittedly, but when you are buying a specific view, you just might need glazing, and air conditioning is the only way to guarantee freshness. And what glazing! Everything from roofs, ceilings, floors, and walls of glass graciously follows the geometry of the steep site. At the entrance the ceiling begins its slope at 9ft (2.7m) and ends at 18ft (5.5m). Without these sloping ceilings, Voorsanger quips, "it would be like seeing a beautiful person up to the top of their knees."

The utterly urbane interior has mahogany floors and ceilings, sourced from tree farms, and an immense French limestone fireplace presides over the main room, reaching up to the incline of the ceiling, a sculpture in itself. In this desert abode, in the hands of interior designer Eve Robinson, the furniture could be from a broad base, since the harsh elements do not enter the house in any manner whatsoever. As for the exits from the house, or rather entries into the wilderness, famed Phoenix-based landscape designer Steve Martino's goal was "to walk out of every door and right into the desert." He disturbed little of the environment, edited plants to little trails, and created and colored retaining walls to mimic the form of the house. "Borrowing vistas is a Japanese trick," he muses. "We made it look as if the whole mountain is theirs."

LEFT Disturbing the environment to a minimal extent, the curve of the roof echoes that of the hillside. At the same time, it stamps a clear identity.

RIGHT On the north side a small pool and terrace were carved from the earth, and the drive and new road were built to the south.

Desert labyrinth
For the Moroccan residence built from scratch for a Paris-based client in an unpopulated wasteland of a site toward the Atlas Mountains from the city of Marrakech, KO architects—Karl Fournier and Olivier Marty—have configured a superb blend of Marrakech architecture and materials with contemporary discipline, mentality, and experience. Despite its magnificence and its nod to Le Corbusier, this is a cozy home.

ABOVE LEFT Natural materials are used in abundance: mixtures of earth, plaster, and straw. Fireplaces inside are clad in metal. Floors are concrete base, then covered with anthracite-colored concrete that has been varnished.

ABOVE The main living rooms on the ground floor level are *enfilade*, in true French manner. The interior remains in penumbra. All furniture has been custom-designed for the house by the architects, lighting likewise.

The architects, their company formed in 2000 (they met at the École des Beaux-Arts in 1996), have achieved quite an impact in Marrakech and set up an office there—their first being in Paris—with ongoing work for such clients as the Hermès family, who have had a presence in Morocco for decades. KO have been responsible for a 1930s Moorish colonial house in Essaouira, ancient Berber restorations, and (with Gae Aulenti) a 30-acre (12ha) property for the Agnelli family. They also designed the award-winning Bo Zin restaurant outside the Medina; all a far cry from chi-chi Parisian restaurants or refurbisments of Haussmanian apartments.

On this 15-acre (6ha) site, the clients wanted a house for weekends and vacations with their four children, teenaged and younger. The family group became the focus for the architects, who built an articulation of "cells" along one side of the principal area, each with its own miniature courtyard, one per child. Its uniformity evokes a rigorous Corbusian manner. Also in the vernacular of Le Corbusier (think Villa Savoye), the children's bathroom

is open plan, four cubicles making up the washing and shower area. In the corridor linking the four cells, four single washbasins jut pertly from the wall. This house is based partly on numbers, partly on passion.

The main dwelling, at a right angle to the children's quarters (they have their own lawned garden, too), consists of an *enfilade* of grander-scaled rooms, for relaxing and dining. Upstairs is the master bedroom suite, with a view over the Atlas Mountains (in winter—in summer, there is a haze) and the most barren panorama imaginable of desert and a few palms. "We are bringing palms into the property now," says the owner, a glamorous figure of a man who nevertheless doesn't mind dipping his feet in soil. The drive to

LEFT A double-height structure—or a tall building—of earth or adobe is structurally impossible, but can be delightful in a hot climate for air movement. In order to build a tall property, KO architects used structural concrete beams as support for the earth walls.

THIS PAGE Rugs are mainly Moroccan from the Atlas Mountains or Berber—wool has a capacity for keeping cool in the summer and warm in the winter. Soft seating is made from pigskin.

PLAN The house, which is approached from the rear, faces the Atlas Mountains. The structure is the only building visible – barren land lies beyond it. Olives and palms, on the whole imported, line the perimeter of the site.

the main door leads past the children's quarter, the house unfolding later on—a demure arrival into a large property, unlike a huge front door and bells chiming magnificence. I would rather experience unfolding pleasures.

At the opposite end of the building, a group of small detached cubes form guest suites, masterful in contemporary simplicity. Outdoor relaxation areas, one an arbor with a planted bamboozerie and one on the roof, are shaded by dried palm leaves and white cotton drapes.

From outside, the walls are almost the color of the ground, not the pinker tone more usually seen locally: soil was brought in from another region to alter the color so the house appears as a mirage. (There is nothing around at all—our directions were to turn off the road at a Coca Cola sign and look for a building.) This is a modern house made of ancient materials. The walls, so thick that heat cannot possibly permeate, are raw-earth brick (comprising earth, straw, and various minerals), pressed and then sun-dried. The exterior is coated in rough earth and straw, interior walls in polished earth and straw, stablized with oil. Ceilings are a plaster-earth mix.

Floors are concrete, varnished with anthracite-colored concrete, which is also on walls and ceilings in the bathrooms. Concrete is used, too, for structural beams, permitting creation of large rooms—double height for air circulation—which would have been almost impossible with only earth.

Because of the intense, overhead sunlight, the windows are narrow, elongated slits, allowing in just shafts of light and little heat; the only large opening is to the south, with a view to the mountains. Rooms remain in penumbra, their darkness enhanced by the dark tones of the walls.

Doors and furniture make use of iroko wood, chestnut, and iron, all simply waxed. Fireplaces and Berber rugs in natural, undyed wools (the black diamond pattern is from black sheep) provide warmth. Curiously, on those rare occasions when the fire is lit, the mountains are reflected in the glass of one of the fireplaces, the snow "melting" in the fire. Fournier admits this was an accident, but very little else appears accidental. Primitive this is not: for two young architects it is a magnificent *oeuvre*.

ABOVE The pool is a welcome respite at any time of day in the desert. The air is exceedingly dry, and it is very easy to dehydrate. Any water feels refreshing. Here you feel as if you are away from civilization for good.

ABOVE CENTER The four children's quarters, in strict uniformity (each child has a small integral terrace). Exterior walls are made from sun-dried raw-earth bricks, finished with a coating of straw and rough earth..

ABOVE RIGHT Inside a child's bedroom. Each child has two beds in case they have a guest. As well as a row of washbasins, there is a shower room in the children's wing. Inside is for sleeping and outdoors for playing.

RIGHT Roof terraces remain the coolest spot for evening dining, although this ground-level relaxation and dining area gives some respite from daytime sun. The Atlas Mountains are just beyond but cannot be seen in high-summer haze.

Fair game

"It is not easy installing a new Africa into Africa," says designer Andrzej Zarzycki, "but the mere commissioning of local pieces and materials from local weavers means that we have an authentic, although quite sophisticated, interior." The exterior, a game farm in the South African bush, takes care of itself.

When lengthy driving directions include the words, "Drive on for about 60 miles [100 km], you will eventually see a green sign: slow down, you are almost there," you know you are in the wild. Once on the property, the vast scale is still apparent, with a good ten-minute drive to the house, visible from the road at times, high up on the hill. Along the road, zebra, kudu, and giraffe pop in and out of sight.

The private game farm (where big game are raised for viewing) in the Northern Province on the road to Thabazimbi that London-based interior designer Andrzej Zarzycki has had the pleasure of creating with his clients contains a host of buildings: dwellings for support staff—gamekeepers, trackers, house staff—as well as a second (or third or fourth) home for the well-traveled and exuberant clients. There are two principal Zarzycki-designed buildings: the main house, built in collaboration with architect

Colin Milliken, which takes the form of a grouping of guest cottages (simple sleep cells feature greatly in hot houses, since most of the living is outdoors; here each bedroom has its own sitting room and bathroom), winging one way and then the other from a central core where entertaining takes place ; and, along a dirt track, another very chic but smaller house, which offers respite for the host from energetic guests and omnipresent animal life— although it too has its share of visitors, as vervet monkeys dramatically appear at the small house's pool each morning and giraffe stroll close by.

Zarzycki is partner to Anthony Collett in the practice Collett-Zarzycki, a 15-year-old architecture and design firm with a 25-strong team as well as a network of outside specialists, artists, and craftspeople. Both partners seek to embrace local tradition wherever they can. Zarzycki grew up in Zambia and knows the sights and sounds of Africa well although, having trained and practiced mainly in Europe, this is his first game-farm project.

The property was originally a 5,000-acre (2,000ha) cattle farm, half on flat land and half in the hills. The owner, on finding his own slice of South Africa, decided to stock it with non-predatory animals so he and his wife and family could safely walk around without the threat of wild cats.

This house is not designed to impress and makes no fanfare; the experience is the property as a whole—the view across the plain beneath and the game watching. "If you remove the house from the terrain, it is not

OPPOSITE Looking into the main sitting room from the deck. Entry to the house is to the right beyond the African mahogany cabinets. The property is high on a hill and fires are needed on cooler evenings: there is a stone hearth in the center of the far wall.

ABOVE Looking from the main sitting room out to the deck, and beyond it the dining room and, to the right, a breakfast and "sundowner" terrace. Furniture in local woods is designed by Collett-Zarzycki, and raffia, here as lampshades (left), is used throughout. Raffia curtains segregating indoors from outdoors are handmade by local craftswomen.

FAR LEFT Some guest suites have outdoor fireplaces. Thatch is used for roofing as it provides good insulation, keeping out summer heat and trapping it in for winter.

LEFT A series of three descending swimming pools is designed to look as un-manmade as possible, visually linking the different elements of the outside terraces. Baboons tend to join visitors for breakfast, as if it is their own pool!

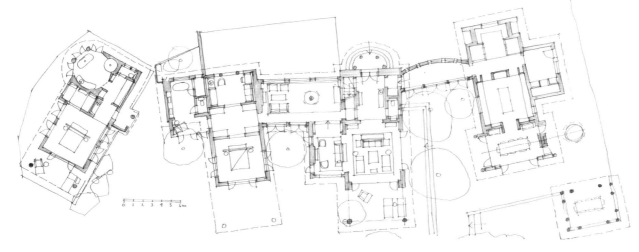

PLAN The house is ostensibly a collection of buildings coming off the main structure. The small buildings act as guest suites. Note the differing orientations of segments for optimal game-watching.

a vast house," comments Zarzycki, "although it does not make sense to remove it since the house is all about the terrain and the mutual acceptance one of the other."

The entrance to the house leads directly into the back of the large south-facing sitting room, with seating arranged to maximize the views through the window wall, which opens entirely onto the deck. The design of the house evolved from its location: it looks outward and is full of wide openings embracing the view. The uninterrupted transition from inside to out succeeds partly because of the choice of upholstered furniture on the deck, which remains year round: the interior and exterior furnishings follow a similar idiom so distinctions between the two are blurred.

Village-like from outside, the units of the house are linked by garden poolside walkways. The series of interlocking rooms flanking the main building are thatched for insulation, keeping out summer heat that reaches 104°F (40°C), and trapping warmth in winter, when temperatures drop to freezing (32°F/0°C). To the north of the house there is a winter room that remains warmer in winter and much lighter than the south-facing side.

Floors throughout the main house are tinted, waxed concrete, while the bedroom cell bathrooms incorporate local granite. Walls are painted pale cream distemper, a good background for the contrasting African dark timbers. "The eye is to be drawn outside so we avoided bright colors in favor of neutrals," says the designer. The client was keen to embrace local materials, but wanted a quality not usually found outside Johannesburg, and it was a challenge working closely with local craftspeople to ensure standards were right, particularly that proportions were adhered to.

Another major challenge was to bring in the amenities, the services, since this was virgin territory. An entirely new drainage system has been set up, with water drawn from boreholes: during periods of drought water is scarce.

Altogether it is a clever house, which at first sight might appear formal. Its informality, however, comes with how it works, its fluidity.

RIGHT Dados in the bathrooms have woven-raffia panels, and basins are built into natural rock. Here the tub is an antique pedestal version; those in other suites are more contemporary resin and stone. Each suite has an alfresco shower, too.

FAR RIGHT All bedrooms open onto separate balconies with long views. Furniture, including contemporary four-poster beds, is by Collet-Zarzycki in stained mahogany. Mohair bedcovers are by Handworks.

OPPOSITE In the double-height winter room is a Zarzycki-designed table of gum-tree poles bound with rope, with a leather-covered top. Campaign chairs in tan leather are a smart addition to this modern Africanate room. Ceiling fans are invaluable in the heat.

wooded

Perhaps the best surroundings for hot homes are trees. Wooded terrain provides relatively instant solutions to some of the problems of living in overheated climes, offering shade from the onslaught of an overhead sun, shelter against strong winds, a degree of moisture in the air and perhaps even rainfall, and a pleasingly soothing sylvan backdrop for hot, sleepy living. What better sounds as you drift into siesta than the rustling of leaves and the chatter of birds?

The humidity that often accompanies woodland, however, is a mixed blessing: in a humid climate there is no shortage of water, and few problems persuading a garden to grow or creating a cooling water feature, but while we might expect moisture to cool us down, in fact high humidity levels make heat a great deal more enervating and can create a sense of airlessness, as well as exposing building materials to punishing rates of rot, mold, rust, and general decay. These are major challenges, requiring targeted solutions and careful choices. Breezes are also an issue, to the extent that simply maintaining a balance between air-conditioned comfort and natural enjoyment of the rainforest environment can be a delicate balancing act.

Fortunately, while forests are inevitably more humid than sparsely vegetated areas, even in hot climates they need not be steaming jungles. Of the homes featured here, one is situated in the humid but not overly hot rainforest of New Zealand's North Island while the other two are both located in the manmade rainforestlike setting of a relatively dry location: Johannesburg, high on the plateau grassland of the South African veld.

However humid it may be, forest does provide another challenge—how not to disturb its natural beauty, or indeed fell at all, despite the temptation of on-the-spot building materials. If the site is truly in the depths of a forest, access to roads and utilities may be almost impossible without cutting a scarring swathe through the trees. Architecture in wooded terrain must also be careful not to fight the trees that surround it. Orientation is not as much of an issue as in other terrains, but postioning vis-à-vis the trees is important, both aesthetically and because roots can be disruptive to foundations. It is usually best to use indigenous materials—although true in all climates, this is particularly so in forests because local materials will cope well with moisture: wood or stone brought in from elsewhere is likely to be too porous. Coming from rainforest environments, tropical hardwoods such as teak are especially suited to hot, humid conditions, while other woods—for instance cedar—smell wonderful when hot, whether damp or dry.

Although builds in forests and woods are problematic, they can be the most beautiful for the play of light through the trees. If you can't build in a forest, you can at least capture something of it by building near a few trees, or planting your own. Under a leafy arbor on a hot morning, the temperature can be ten degrees cooler than in the sun. Even in deserts there is that age-old symbol of oasis, the palm tree. When planting palms, be aware that many species cannot tolerate extreme conditions. My personal favourite, the Queen Palm, does badly in cold winters: only fortunate people who live in Palm Springs and other warm-winter areas can enjoy its beauty year round. Palms are essentially architectural. As they mature, many become tall brown columns topped with a giant powder-puff of green. In the long term, shorter palms are generally better for a hint of shade in a hot garden.

OPPOSITE Clifford Forsyth House is a rigorous structure in a leafy New Zealand suburb. Apart from the two angled concrete-block walls that bring shade and privacy, the house consists of thin, laminated wood posts and great expanses of glass infill, a transparency that invites in the trees and belies the suburban location.

Ultimate wood cabin

Arguably one of the most significant houses created in New Zealand in the 20th century is the home architect Patrick Clifford designed for himself in an Auckland suburb. Clifford Forsyth House is built on interesting topography on a sloping triangular plot that ends at a tidal basin. Showing huge courtesy to its environment and appearing essentially made from wood, it is of human scale and compassionate content. Clifford explains: "The built environment plays a major role in the human impact on natural environment and quality of life.... A sustainable design integrates consideration of resource and energy efficiency, healthy buildings and materials, ecologically and socially sensitive land use, and aesthetic sensitivity."

If there is a New Zealand vernacular, this house is its contemporary epitome. But is there one? In the first years of the 21st century, evidence to suggest ongoing development of a local domestic architecture in New Zealand is sparse. Yet the belief that a uniquely and recognizably New Zealand house might exist was first established as a cultural discussion-point a hundred years ago on the cusp of the 20th century, when it hardly mattered that there was little physical evidence. However, by the 1940s, urged on by the centenary of the signing of the Treaty of

ABOVE LEFT All rooms act as viewing platforms for the wooded scenery. Privacy is achieved thanks to surrounding mature plantings and uneven land. Wooden shutters control sunlight here, with adjustable glass louvers for air circulation throughout.

ABOVE The design concept began with an investigation of the relationship between a light wooden frame and solid retaining block walls and an ideal of creating a boathouse-like retreat within the city— as exemplified in this dining area.

RIGHT Semi-opaque glass provides visual contrast to the transparency of the house. Folding doors to the deck open flush to expose the great outdoors. Entrance is via descending steps down the slope of the site to this courtyard, which also acts as a terrace.

Waitangi (which had brought peace between the Maori chiefs and the British crown) and the nationalism that tends to accompany wars, triggered by the onset of World War II, New Zealand architects began to pay more attention to the built manifestation of the "Kiwi" house. (My husband is a Kiwi, his father a property developer from Christchurch, so I do feel somewhat qualified to comment on their built environment.) The first example to achieve widespread acceptance as a typical style was a small house built during the summer of 1949 by Group Construction, later renamed Group Architects.

This was the first of many built in the late 1940s and the 1950s which led to establishment of the characteristics of the "typical" New Zealand house that have been applied since. The criteria (not an issue of style, more a democratic and egalitarian thrust) were that it should modest in scale, innovative in its design and within affordable reach. Last, it should be made from wood, although true consideration for the environment came later. Eventually postwar "builders," probably perceiving timber as unsophisticated, disguised it behind wallboard or brick veneers. Architects, on the other hand, inclined to the experimental, exploring exposed timber as siding, floorboards, wall linings, and ceilings. Latterly on the South Island, architects added other materials and adapted wood in recognition of climatic variation. By the 1970s, what had started out as a list of principles had resulted in a real style. In the late 1940s architecture had been tied to the ongoing affordability of wood, and pine forests planted during the Depression powered timber architecture well into the 1980s. Yet by the time the North Island's Clifford Forsyth House was completed, timber costs had escalated, and it may turn out to be one of the last houses of its type.

Architectus, one of New Zealand's eminent contemporary architectural practices, has made a major contribution to the changing face of the New Zealand built environment. Started more than 20 years ago by Patrick Clifford (who graduated as an architect in 1981), Malcolm Bowes, and Michael Thomson, Architectus has won just about every New Zealand Institute of Architects award for architecture, and many of their buildings have become New Zealand's modern architectural icons. Recently moving into the international arena, the practice has joined with a group of Australian architects to form offices elsewhere with connections to other practices around the world. Today Architectus brings together the experience of more than 160 leading architects, designers and planners, with offices in Auckland, Brisbane, Melbourne, Sydney, and Shanghai.

Despite his very worthy accolades, and larger builds, Clifford remains a memorable house designer. I cannot help but wonder if in recent years the socialist ambitions of the original wooden-house designers have been subverted into the production of a new cultural product, the architect-designed house as a rich person's plaything—although not, of course, in the case of this house, with its rigorous structure and calmly unpretentious mood. In New Zealand, as in Australia, we continue to see a move from architectural egalitarianism to architectural elitism (note the shift of contemporary architecture from the suburb to the beach), and I only hope it is not a permanent one.

LEFT The units of the kitchen, which defines one side of the open-plan living/dining space, follow the angled wall.

BOTTOM FAR LEFT The frame and walls of the 2,690sq ft (250sq m) house sit on a concrete base, while a folded plate roof, underlined with plywood, tops it all off. The approach is from the street above.

BOTTOM CENTER Use of wood can be modern. According to the architect, "environmental ethics means full understanding of the ecological interdependence of the development."

BOTTOM LEFT Generally for the past century the architect-designed New Zealand house has been wooden. Here ceiling joists are exposed and the staircase has an open-grille balustrade.

SKETCH The house has three storys. The main floor is in the middle, with guest suites below and two bedrooms and a bathroom upstairs. Decks are cantilevered.

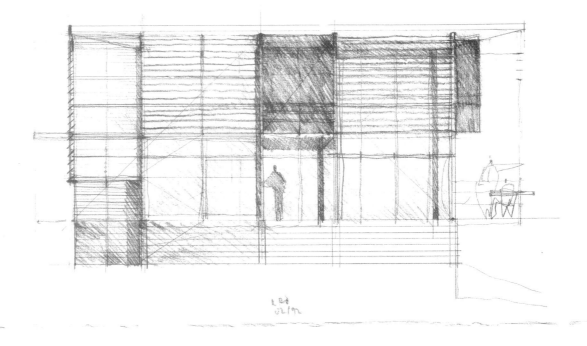

Forest lair
Embedded in a Johannesburg hillside, South African architect Johann Slee's home treats the surrounding forest as not only its garden, but even part of the house, blurring the moment between inside and out. A solid cliff-like structure, it opens up like caves into the tree canopy. "The forest is a stage set," says the architect.

Unlike his European counterparts, Slee designs more residences than any other kind of building. In Europe, architects tend to survive through commercial projects and space is rare (helpful land and building laws rarer still). Twelve houses is the average per year in Johannesburg alone for Slee and his small team. The delightful "treehouse" he has built as his own home nestles in the forest in Westcliff, one of Johannesburg's oldest suburbs, and is paean to environmentally conscious building.

The plot, originally 1 acre (0.4ha), as are most in the area, has been reduced by half (the other half is rented to another architect). The house, a labyrinth of corridors and rooms that billow at you on approach, was built up and down using the footprint of the previous, much smaller and humbler 1960s house, home of the illustrator who designed the South African currency, the rand, in 1961 when the South African pound was replaced by the newer currency to reflect the new republic's birth. Slee, an Afrikaner, rather enjoys knowing the previous place housed an artist since he paints, too. Ever fond of history, he quips of South Africa, "The British built the roads and the Dutch built the houses.... Both were very good at it—the British created a good infrastructure and the Dutch added vision."

ABOVE LEFT The principal living room, at entry level, where vast metal shutters draw back to open the sunny, north-facing front of the house to the forest. Walls are pigmented earth and cement mixed; the green seat has been adapted from an Indian platform used for sitar playing.

ABOVE The metal-framed door leads from the living room to this outdoor room cantilevered over the hillside. Chairs are Arts and Crafts steamer style. The outdoor fireplace makes the space cozier.

RIGHT The approach to the house is along a sandstone footbridge to the main door (right of shot). Dry-packed stone walls, characteristic of the suburb, were used as the main design element.

FAR RIGHT Slee's studio is south-facing (remember this is the southern hemisphere: the sun is to the north), at the very rear of the house. "The light here has a magnificent spell," he says. The clarity of light is already spectacularly good in Johannesburg, which is 5,740ft (1,750m) above sea level.

The site is on a hill, so instead of shipping in materials to build, the architect set about mining the land, and all building materials have come directly from the ground beneath. The house, which sinks deep into the ground, rises high above it, too, with walls of windows on every face and at every level so that you feel as if you are living entirely with the surrounding nature, transported into the forest at every turn—birds even fly through the house. The most magnificent achievement in this build is the cantilevered room which shares two walls with the main living space but is exposed on the other two sides. A far cry from a terrace or deck, the room is dressed with Arts and Crafts steamer chairs and leather sofas arranged around the hearth. It really is hard to know whether you are inside or out.

The build was difficult, Slee admits, due to limited space for construction with the mining happening simultaneously, and because, using dry stone and adobe materials, despite his usual rectilinear passions, he couldn't seem to produce a right angle anywhere in the building, so he just let the odd bend happen. "Some materials do not behave exactly as you wish, and this is not a shoebox-shaped house," he says. "Building with natural materials means following its imperfections."

Johannesburg, being inland and 5,740ft (1,750m) above sea level, is not naturally humid. However, trees (often imported) have been planted widely to create a local "rainforest," refreshing for its moisture and shade. As the architect notes, not without some irony, "With the newfound Africanization of South Africa, which I support, some of the trees in my garden might be contraband soon and may have to make way for real indigenous species, but my wife and I believe that all the trees surrounding the property have a

LEFT An enormous metal-framed door forms the overture to the house: note the runner in the stone floor to enable a door of such weight to swing with ample support. Its opening appears as yet another picture window.

RIGHT There is a brutal element to this house, built from stone mined from the property (no transportation expense) so that it could be set deep into the hillside in the void created by mining. Supporting "I" beams are exposed, yet walls show the touch of the hand and are made from old "recipes."

right to be here, whether brought in by Europeans or native to the land." Slee's elegant wife, Rene, a magazine journalist specializing in gardens and flowers, is responsible alongside her husband for the interior of the house.

The gate from the road opens onto a contemporary sandstone rail-less bridge which, fixed to the property wall (in the same compacted dry stone as the house exterior and some interior walls), leads to the house, visible in its entirety only from this angle. A bathtub-like pool sits directly in front of the house, coming at you vertically and visually augmenting the linear nature of the house's height. The massive double-width main door is to the right and the principal space visible to the left, along a corridor where glass walls reveal an uphill cottage garden.

On the main, upper floor, the open-plan space still manages pockets as rooms, since the property is so vast: the kitchen and its long refectory table, a further dining area which precedes the outdoor room, all are in total harmony in their earthen and brown hues, the green form outside omnipresent, but very different emotionally and material-wise. In the kitchen dining area, for example, steel "I" beams hold the structure in place and visually give an industrial feel, yet a more boutique mood is given by light shafting through square holes that have become skylights.

Below, on a mezzanine level, are master bedroom and bath and shower, while one full level down provides den and bedrooms for the children, off a wide corridor that doubles as a family room, as well as guest rooms (the Slees seem to have adopted some permanent guests, a colorful array of friends). Windows at every facet give view to the vistas outside. Even guest shower and wet rooms have long, narrow slit windows, floor to ceiling, so bathers can feel the breeze and be at one with the flora beyond. Toward the very back of the house, at its lowest point, is the studio where Johann paints. His practice office is also on the property, a self-contained unit.

I think Slee's rigid architectural training and his deep fascination for art have combined beautifully to produce a very painterly home for his family. It has been built with passion, without disrupting anyone else's terrain, using the spoils of his own land—even the wood used in the interior and pieces of furniture such as the tables have used wood from the structure of the previous dwelling—and deserves status as an example to all.

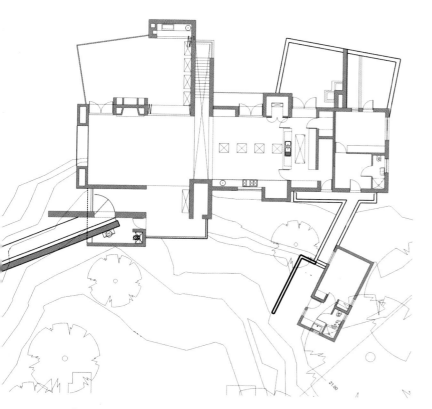

PLAN The principal, upper floor features the bridge, interior and exterior living rooms (left) and the kitchen, hub of the house. Downstairs are two floors of bedrooms, a den, and bathrooms. The connected smaller building is for staff.

Urban bush camp idyll

Proponents of natural living and handcrafted local skills, South African husband-and-wife architect team Silvio Rech and Lesley Carstens have built their own Johannesburg home to resemble a group of *rondavels*, or mud huts. "We create a true Africa in most of our projects," claims Rech.

Situated nearly 350 miles (560km) from the nearest port, on a vast inland plateau, 5,700ft (1,700m) above sea level, Johannesburg's climate is much milder and drier than its latitude would suggest. Sub-Saharan Africa's greatest city, it straddles rows of quartzite ridges, beneath which a century of gold mining produced a veritable honeycomb of tunnels. In Zulu, Johannesburg is called E'goli ("place of gold"), an epithet no longer quite fitting as the last of the mines ran out of gold-bearing ore decades ago. The towering yellow mine dumps have largely been recycled, and today numerous trees rise from the sprawling suburbs, so that on

OPPOSITE The lofty circular bedroom sleeps the family of four, with an elevated double bed providing a view into the garden through a roof-to-floor glass double door. Under the bed are two built-in beds for the children, safely tucked under their parents.

LEFT, TOP The bathroom has a few mod cons and a contemporary concept of "his and hers" washbasins, yet remains in the African vernacular.

LEFT, BOTTOM Thatching has great insulation properties and behaves well in hot weather. It also helps a building to merge into a forest. Note the white Vernor Panton chair on the deck.

RIGHT, ABOVE Roofs are vaulted and look down onto polished concrete floors. Small oval windows allow just enough light for good vision, but keep the interior cool. Carstens and Rech design anything from soft furnishings to door handles, but always with a sense of Africa, its rich textures and tones.

satellite images much of Johannesburg resembles a rainforest, an unexpected backdrop to an array of Victorian and Edwardian architecture, as well as concrete, chrome, and glass skyscrapers.

Prior to 1993, Silvio Rech and Lesley Carstens's works were of a modern nature, mainly in large cities in South Africa. Since then, however, they have been developing a "hand-crafted *haute couture*" body of work in Africa, and have created numerous award-winning bush camps, published widely. But they cannot be called traditionalists since their youth and rigorous architecture training has afforded them many skills beyond simply building the old-fashioned way. Part of the design philosophy has been to live on site in exotic locations, doing one project at a time, developing a total design and creating a new language of architecture and a lifestyle particular to each situation. Most of their projects have included an element of transfer of skills to the local African communities from the core team of builders that they've gathered from all over Africa.

I first discovered their work at North Island, Seychelles, a private island hideaway-cum-eco-Noah's Ark in the turquoise waters of the Indian Ocean. The main lodge, designed by the South African architects, dramatizes the Seychelles' ancient role as a crossroads of Asian, Indian, and African cultures. Rech and Carstens worked with a team of craftsmen from Africa, Zanzibar, Bali, and the Seychelles to create a fusion of cultures and architectural styles. The team seeks to incorporate elements that remind visitors to all their projects just what natural living is about—and hot living: thatched *alang alang* roofs, *punkah punkah* fans, and fully retracting sliding windows (for 270-degree views) providing a pampering environment for the enjoyment of the balmy conditions they are fortunate enough to work with.

FAR LEFT The open-plan bathroom has a sunken bath, copper-wire light, and ocher walls. The lavatory is doorless, too.

LEFT & RIGHT In the office-cum-dining room (when clients come; otherwise, dining is alfresco) new furniture designs are on show, including a plastic-tube chandelier and sheer fabric screen for bedrooms in the Okavango Delta. The blond wood bench seat and table were custom-designed for the project and will eventually go into production. Note the tree growing up through the roof.

Once within the gates of their own enclosed property, an acre precisely (0.4ha), their signature style is apparent. As architects and interior architects, their home is a "total work of art," with every nook and cranny custom-designed. Explains Rech, "Our clients visit us here and this is what they expect to see. It is also how we are used to living," he adds as his two small children gambol about, in and out of the buildings, splashing in a pond for a moment before creating a psychodrama that occupies them outdoors for hours. The peripatetic lifestyle is feasible with small children who adapt.

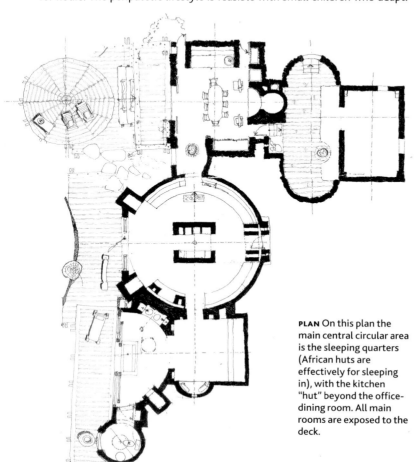

PLAN On this plan the main central circular area is the sleeping quarters (African huts are effectively for sleeping in), with the kitchen "hut" beyond the office-dining room. All main rooms are exposed to the deck.

Although superficially the house resembles several thatched-roofed *rondavels*, with a long multi-level deck that overlooks the lush overgrown garden which contains numerous lily ponds, a separate wine cellar, and a trampoline, beneath the surface is a home of unusual warmth and captivating traditional and modern design. The "house" consists of one large interleading structure, part of it the living area, the other part for sleeping. The walls of the living area are of sandstone with built-in wooden shelves and a tree growing into the roof between the two main rooms.

Off the bedroom, via a dressing room, is a large, luxurious sunken bath overlooking the garden, and a doorless lavatory "cubicle," as open to the elements as the rest of the bathroom. Like the bedroom, the bathroom is heated by means of fireplaces, whose flames flicker around walls finished in rich brown mud. The roof is vaulted, finished in brick, and looks down onto a concrete floor. The textures are many: the mix of sandstone and rough ocher walls backdrop decorative skulls collected in the bush and strips of white pebbles on the floor. "The materials become the buildings," Rech explains, giving as an example chairs that are made of logs, or boulders that are like chairs. "You can sit on the boulder or the chair."

These enviable architects have duplicated their unique style of luxury in African bush lodges not only in South Africa, but also in parts of Tanzania, Mozambique, and the Okavango Delta in Botswana. In addition, they are building a lodge in Portugal and a home in Greece. "We get a call every day from a different country," Rech says, promising not to waiver from his dedication to the environment as he imbibes the local culture, incorporates elements of it into a design, and continues to support local craftspeople. According to his wife, incidentally an extremely fit Olympic rower, "He wanders around with ideas all the time, then finds a site for them."

But in case you think this life is just too idyllic, bear in mind that the couple are heavily involved in the creative industries' Capetown-based Design Indaba, which holds an annual event now popular worldwide. The local *Weekly Mail and Guardian* applauded what they called Indaba's "visceral" mission statement: "Fed up with the dead-end prospects of an economy reliant on basic commodities, its ambitious roadmap outlines a creative design industry as the beating heart of both society and the economy…. Rather than pouring our efforts into large-scale, pollution-causing industries, it advocates leap-frogging on the experience of the First World and becoming a creative services hub for the entire planet."

cultivated

A cultivated terrain can be a clipped and manicured garden or a rambling vineyard. It can even mean a desert garden, or structural landscaping around a property. Despite their diversity, such surroundings have a number of elements in common. The soil has been worked in some form or other, and basic amenities have probably been laid on. When it comes to building a home, there is more ease of access but less freedom of design than in a wilderness, but fewer constraints than in an urban landscape.

In dealing with the issues of heat and intense sunshine, a cultivated terrain faces similar problems to other regions—although worst extremes of aridity or humidity are rare, since these would not allow cultivation in the first place—but the building restrictions that go with living in a relatively developed area may mean that the easiest solutions are not acceptable, and cooling and power-generating mechanisms may have to return to older ways, such as including a subterranean level, to avoid clashing with neighbors' needs or sightlines. On the other hand, the landscaping and planting of a garden, or existing foliage, can often be made to help with requirements such as shade.

Architecturally, there is significantly less freedom than in many other circumstances. In some parts of the South of France, especially Provence, local building regulations are so strict that in effect nothing is allowed other than relatively low-level, traditional-looking structures that echo the vernacular and are absolutely certain not to interfere with the ambience of their surroundings. Even where constraints are not so tight, a cultivated environment tends to be gentler, and new builds need to take care not to dwarf their surroundings with dramatic statements. As a result, many people choose to restore an old building, keeping their modern impulses for the interior.

Creativity in a cultivated area often goes as much into landscaping and designing a garden, the immediate environs, as the house. In hot climates, in any case, the line between indoor and outdoor tends to blur: the garden is part of the living space. When cultivating land in such a climate, the need for water must be approached responsibly, and it is important to remember that things can go wrong quickly in the heat. Planning a landscape design can also be very different from gardening in temperate climates. The weather is different, the soil can be difficult, and plants often seem alien.

Hot deserts are home to some striking plants and fragile, beautiful ecosystems, although these vary according to soil, altitude, and rainfall. Cacti and succulents are the ultimate drought-tolerant plants: they absolutely love the sun and require infrequent watering. A number of striking plants originating from the tropics, including agaves, bird-of-paradise plants, and the red-flowered ocotillo, do well in hot-desert homes in North America. Then there is mesquite, a mimosa-like tree that provides good shade on minimal water. Other than the autumn litter of seedpods and invasive roots (avoid planting near plumbing pipes), they are handsome and characteristic of North American deserts.

Vines and olives conjure a different kind of hot garden. The olive, a Mediterranean classic that defines many a garden, offers welcome cool shade in summer. Perhaps most effective of all, even in dry climates—not to mention the bonus of culinary use—are aromatic herbs such as rosemary, thyme, and marjoram or oregano. Rosemary is particularly adaptable to different conditions, and smells wonderful, another benefit of cultivated surroundings.

OPPOSITE A foliage-filled court backs onto a house in Kyalami, South Africa, by Johann Slee. The house, built for entertaining, is positioned on a circular pivot-irrigation seedling platform of a redundant plant nursery.

Nice story

A Provençal dream of a small house, the joint work of several designers, combines modern skills and local authenticity. As designer Andrzej Zarzycki explains, "Living outside is natural and what we love: protecting ourselves from extreme sun, rain, wind, all the elements, is why we need architecture, and using inside/outside devices brings us even closer to living in nature."

French Riviera properties seem to come in two guises: either fabulous 1960s and '70s apartments overlooking the Mediterranean (think Bridget Bardot and Peter Sellers) or typical inland Provençal houses made from local stone. In the latter case, there are tight building restrictions in the area, particularly in the countryside, and many a house builder has had "condemned" stamped upon a beloved property before the paint has had time to dry. There seems therefore to be a career to be made in the region for a true professional, which is exactly what Scottish architect Robert Dallas has done. Dallas appears to have a monopoly on building in the Provençal style, and he does it very well. So interior designer Andrzej Zarzycki, from London firm Collett-Zarzycki, called upon Dallas to assist with a commission from trusted longterm clients.

The clients already owned an old house in the area but, because of the size of their land, managed to obtain permission to build another on the property. The original stone house is exquisite, but with a burgeoning family and possibly aware of being in their *troisième age* as the French say, they were keen to downsize a little (they spend only a couple of months in France per year), move into the new house, and let the family take over the rambling original building.

A short drive from Nice, the picturesque 13th-century village of St Paul de Vence is a delightful milieu for a home, an area steeped in history. It is a fortified village perched on a narrow spur between two deep valleys and home to a true artistic treat, the remarkable Fondation Maeght, created in the 1950s by Aimé and Marguerite Maeght, art collectors and dealers who knew all the great artists in the region. (Inside the gates, witness Alberto Giacometti's *Cat* stalking along the edge of the grass, Miró's *Egg* smiling above a pond and his totemic *Fork* outlined against the sky. A Calder mobile swings over watery tiles, by Léger's *Flowers, Birds and a Bench* on a sunlit rough stone wall, and a tubular fountain

FAR LEFT Although created within the grounds of an existing house, the garden has been designed and cultivated anew, by garden designer Jean Mus. Lavender and olive trees set the tone for a dusty yet verdant landscape.

LEFT A small dining room sits just within the boundaries of the house: all rooms lead directly outside. Art plays a large part in the addition of color into the otherwise neutral palette. Paintings throughout are by British artist Ian McKeever.

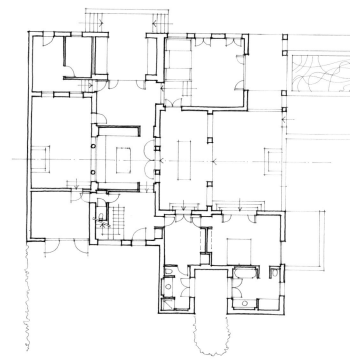

PLAN Different levels have been created, although very carefully so there is no abruptness. The bottom of this plan shows the highest ground level, while at the pool level (top right) the house is at its lowest.

by Pol Bury clanks away.) The other famous sight in this bustling village is La Colombe d'Or hotel, on whose walls you can enjoy Braques, Picassos, Matisses, and Bonnards, most of them acquired by the establishment in the lean post-World War I years in lieu of the artists' unpaid bills. Another arty fact: Russian-born painter Marc Chagall is buried in the cemetery there, too! The village itself is one of the most intact medieval examples of the region, with much of the ramparts still there, so in building just a few miles along the road, it is important to respect the local architectural vernacular.

The same applies to the high standard of horticulture. True, the region has its olive groves and lavender, but there are also fantastic cultivated

gardens, mainly private, that are world class. Again, not wanting to upset the neighbors, Zarzycki and his clients had famed landscape designer Jean Mus, who works exclusively with indigenous plants, design the entire garden. It was developed in a very organized manner: the design and hard landscaping was done during construction, planting right at the end. "Since the house was built a year or two ago, it has filled out but has remained essentially the same," says the designer.

The house itself, which has a footprint of around 3,200sq. ft (300sq m), has thick walls for insulation. "It was also important to create through drafts," says Zarzycki. "This house has no air conditioning. Where we have large glazed areas, we have tried to incorporate overhanging roofs to minimize solar heat gain via the glass."

In the region there is a restriction on house height of 23ft (7m), so as not to obscure the landscape, which is quite a challenge on a hilly site. Different levels have been created carefully here so there is no abruptness: the flow is seamless. The designer says he would have preferred one level, "but the site slopes so in order to obtain larger volumes we dropped floor levels." The thick walls are local stone—*cine*—and floors are reclaimed terracotta tiles. All internal carpentry is in oak (an indigenous material) and metalwork is hand-forged iron, "which kept both French and English ironworkers quite busy." Zarzycki feels a responsibility to the artisan industries and pledges to keep craftsmanship alive—clearly in tune with Provençal thinking.

ABOVE The main suite, seen here, is at ground level. Slightly raised above the other rooms, it is positioned toward the top of the incline. There is also an upstairs, however, which houses the guest bedrooms.

ABOVE RIGHT Stylistically, all new buildings are required to be in keeping with the local vernacular. "Defining outside spaces with walls and geometric planting makes the outside feel like inside, thus a more utilitarian space," says the designer. The pool interior is black.

ABOVE FAR RIGHT The interior features local oak, along with reclaimed floor tiles. The balustrades, in forged iron, were handcrafted in England, although other metalwork came from France.

RIGHT The double-height sitting room has an overhanging roof to keep it

cooler. There are no steps to the outside: "Using similar materials inside and out and maintaining levels between them helps to blur the difference between the two and encourages flow of space." Almost all furniture was custom-designed for the project except two safari-type chairs.

Moroccan modern
Karim El Achak is a modern architect, his Marrakech house a paean to good international architecture, by which I mean it can be understood by many cultures and would work well in any climate where the sun beats down. It is well thought out, cool in summer, and a visual, colorful treat, yet without visual noise.

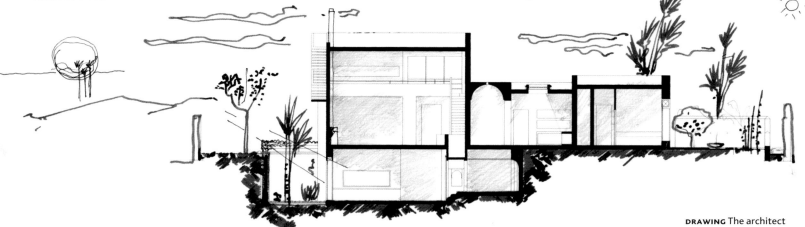

DRAWING The architect has sketched his home in section to include its subterranean level. Subterranean living in a warm climate can only be successful in dry heat. Underground is a family room and an integral mosque, raised slightly. Note the depiction of the sun's movement.

RIGHT El Achak always builds around flora, then cultivates more. Palms in dusty Marrakech are often shifted at whim. His home, here the front, is built on an interesting configuration of axes.

Morocco today is a very different scene from the 1960s hippy destination, with far more to offer than the sights and sounds of the kasbah, medina, and bazaars. It is a journey today's hipsters are making with increasing frequency: tourism is up by 25 percent on average per year, and more and more outsiders are buying property since it offers good potential for growth.

Cosmopolitan Marrakech is the epicenter of the real-estate boom, and it is not much of a surprise any longer to find world-class architects, local or imported, working in the region—and not just in the luxurious Palmeraie area inhabited mainly by French sophisticates. There are barren areas now under construction, including the as yet unsignposted location on the edge of the cultivated suburb of Palmeraie where architect Karim El Achak has elected to build his family home. For insiders and outsiders, the appeal of Morocco goes beyond investment potential. It is a wonderful place to live and bring up children, and probably the most exotic country you can reach within a three-hour flight from many of Europe's cities; its unique decorative style, vibrant culture, and warm year-round climate make it all the more appealing: Marrakech stays at around 68°F (about 20–21°C) in winter and has 300 days of sunshine; it is a dry heat so no problems sleeping at night.

I first came across the work of architect Karim El Achak at a small luxury development just outside Marrakech. A lovely, fertile spot surrounded by cypresses, orange and fig trees, it

FAR LEFT Pigmented exterior walls help to apportion the cultivated garden and block views of less-inspired houses. Marrakech is warm and sunny year-round. We photographed the house in the fall for blue sky: in summer the sky is white.

LEFT The rear of Villa Anjal is the most spectacular façade, huge glazed, metal-framed doors standing like sentries. The swimming pool is deeper by the house so a refreshing dive is achieved without a walk on hot stone. Terraces are local stone.

was full of birdsong and the scent of orange blossom. A true conservationist (of buildings and landscape), El Achak had insisted that most of the trees be preserved, despite the density of the building, and they now produce their own olives, olive oil, and other goodies.

The second time I encountered his work, it was a riad refurbishment in Marrakech: the magnificently rich-looking yet minimalist chic Riad 72. Riads are traditional Moroccan buildings—a house set around a courtyard, with typical features including mosaics, Moorish arches, and often a water feature.

I was delighted when I contacted El Achak for the first time to find he was in the process of completing his own home, which had taken two years to build. With true Moroccan hospitality he invited us to visit, but before we could set foot inside we shared tea and a hearty breakfast. In Morocco, houses seem more revered and people more polite than elsewhere.

Closely involved in the project has been El Achak's wife, an Italian Catholic, whom he met when studying architecture in Italy. They eventually married and returned to Marrakech, where they have been based for 15 years (their two young sons speak equally Italian and Arabic and not-at-all-bad English).

The architect, who is originally from Casablanca and has film-star looks, is quick to describe his work as "inspiring wellbeing" before slipping into the pool for a midday cool-down. The main house is airy and spacious, open on most sides (west only at subterranean level), since the Moroccan sun is so high in the sky that issues such as being "south-facing" simply do not apply. There is also a small single-story traditional Moroccan-style guesthouse in a private plot behind a wall in the garden, its tiny mosaic bathrooms and kitchens reminiscent of riad living.

Entry to the main house, once you have passed the concealed guesthouse, is directly into the living room from the pathway. A lofty, predominantly white room, it has a mezzanine balcony that looks over the main room and has

RIGHT El Achak has created his own art using Moroccan trays. Other artwork, by a local artist, is created using sands of neighboring regions. Door and window frames are black metal, which behaves well in the climate. Furniture is from Moroso, including a T-Phoenix powder-coated steel table by Patricia Urquiola.

typical blackened Moorish screens in the outside wall allowing limited light in and giving a view on the world beyond.

One seating arrangement is also traditional in that, built-in, it sweeps around the perimeter of a seating niche, its cushions padded for luxuriousness and vibrant in gem colors. Around the fireplace is a less traditional seating arrangement, a contemporary sofa and cantilevered tables.

The dining area, the focus of the house, is toward the back, and leads to a terrace and the garden. These contain more Italian contemporary furniture and chairs by award-winning designer Patricia Urquiola. "Being Moroccan doesn't preclude us from the high end of modern design," says the architect with a smile.

Bedrooms are in a separate wing on the ground floor and downstairs, at subterranean level, is a palatial office-TV room and den, or "family room." Just beyond its casual seating is a door, up a couple of steps from floor level, which leads to El Achak's own personal mosque, an absolute treat for anyone's eyes, but out of respect we do not show it here. The elegant and soft-spoken El Achak is a devout Muslim and is educating his children likewise.

Spending much of his time campaigning for responsible redevelopment of the city's historical sites, including a controversial project to conserve a marketplace due for demolition, he exhibits generosity and warmth at work and at home. It was a pleasure to visit. He even insisted I send a taxi to pick up my husband and baby from the hotel in Marrakech so he could extend his hospitality. Within a few minutes they, too, were keeping cool in the pool, which as we watched evaporated inches before our eyes!

OPPOSITE The main entrance is less grand than the rear. Floors are full ceramic porcelain stoneware. Although El Achak has used traditional wall effects such as *tadelak*, where shine is added to pigment, here walls have a modern powdery finish created by painting base onto chalk (only the bathrooms have *tadelak*). The stairs are concrete, and red is used as accent color. Rugs are Berber.

TOP LEFT Landscaping at the front of the house is as geometric as its interior and its footprint.

TOP CENTER Italy-based Spanish designer Patricia Urquiola is a favorite of the couple: dining chairs are Bloomy by Urquiola for Moroso. Red comes to life in winter sunshine (whereas blue is luminous in dimness). As El Achak points out, "The sun does not enter the house at all in summer: the Moroccan sun is too high overhead." Double doors open inward in French manner to bring in any breeze.

TOP RIGHT An outdoor shower peeks from behind a floating wall in the rear garden, and a mature olive tree stands proud. Water is at a premium in the desert, and a garden can be quite an undertaking. The poolside chairs are legless and ultra modern.

ABOVE El Achak's wife, Clara Candido, has a firm that produces handcrafted Moroccan objects for export. Her creative stamp is evident throughout: many fabrics and objects are pieces she has collated. The seating in this niche is a traditional element modernized. The ceiling, by contrast, is highly ornamental.

Vaulting ambition Overlooking verdant vineyards and orchards
near the Adriatic coast of central Italy, a former monastery has been transformed
into a sympathetic home. Architect Paolo Badesco has unified an interior space so
that it is primed for modern living, yet has not lost its historical value and spirit.

Le Marche—touted as the "new Tuscany"—stretches inland from the beach resorts and ports of the Adriatic coastline. With its unspoiled beauty and excellent food and drink, it is the most mysterious of the triumvirate of regions that comprise central Italy (the others being Tuscany and Umbria), except for the weather, which is always balmy in summer and cool in winter—perfect for a seasonal retreat from city life.

If you plan to go to Le Marche (and you should—few visitors penetrate its hinterland), you need to sort out the pronunciation first. Le Marche is pronounced "lay markay." It translates into English as "the Marches" and that's how many of us know it. The scenery is frankly exquisite: approaching the coastal plain, mountains drop to gently rounded hills, often topped with fortified towns a millennium or more old, surrounded by green, fertile slopes of olive groves and vineyards. And then the land drops again to the long, broad, shallow beaches where there are excellent stretches of sand, and then the Conero peninsula, a rugged limestone promontory (limestone is a fantastic building material). As with much of Italy, wine is important to the region, and the classic wine of Marche is Verdicchio, a crisp, young, green-tinged white, excellent with fish and seafood—and since there is plenty of coast, there is plenty of seafood.

So it is no surprise that a canny couple of shoe designers from Milan might choose to have their summer home in Le Marche, far from the madding Tuscan crowds. No surprise also that they should choose a fellow Milanese, architect Paolo Badesco, to help with the restoration of their find.

As you leave the snaking road to the house, which through the vineyards appears as an austere rectangular form in red brick (Italian red brick is much paler than British), you soon become aware of the building's age. Mighty from the outside and demure from within, it was originally a 15th-century monastery, and like the countryside around it, has hidden secrets—not least the sweeping vaulted ceilings that lift and fall as if intonating the space. The staccato vaults, in their soldier uniformity, are almost audible,

BELOW LEFT In the kitchen, windowpanes are recessed directly into the curved wall without frames, for optimum pane area. Chairs are from Cappellini, and the central workstation is stainless steel and Corian from Boffi.

BELOW The Milanese are beginning to choose Le Marche over Tuscany for second homes for peace and quiet. Milan-based architect Badesco was chosen to restore and refurbish the building in a contemporary but sensitive manner.

RIGHT Soft light pours under the low vaulted ceilings. Daylight also bounces off the white floor, almost lighting them up (in olden days the opposite would have been desired: the vaults would have remained dark and mysterious).

their tone softened visually by gentle light from the windows. "Intuitively he understood that the purity of the ceilings called for a rehabilitation that would be sober and contemporary," the owners say of Badesco's approach. The monastic element continues into the selection of tailored furniture and a neutral palette. This is a home for a family with young children, so stark minimalism was not going to work—but peace and serenity does.

The focus of the project was to completely re-cover all the interior surfaces of the house, to create a clean and fluid space, except for interior brickwork which was duly and dutifully washed. A main concern was the floor, which has been completely covered with a white resin containing marble dust that gives it depth and patina. The floor's uniformity gives the home a sense of continuity and visual flow, underlining the structure above.

The architect also "modernized" the house by reapportioning the volumes of the upstairs floor—there are now four substantial bedrooms and larger ultra-chic bathrooms. The parents' bedroom is very sober indeed, the children's more playful, but all have a tranquil spirit.

There are many successes in this very beautifully restored house, but the true heroes are the vistas and views over the deeply undulating clipped countryside where vines and soft fruits grow in abundance. No surprise, therefore, that the kitchen, stuffed with homemade compotes of apricots picked just outside the door, offers prime views through large picture windows. In a region boasting such good food and wine, the kitchen cannot but be the hub of the home. Architecturally the room was a challenge to Badesco, who at first felt it was overly exposed to the elements. The central unit brought the space together (there were no free walls once windows were in place) and the kitchen has now found its identity. This is a time for inspiration in the region, for inserting modernity into ancient, working with extreme features—even exaggerating them—and unifying the rest.

FAR LEFT Ancient pillars are boxed in for visual lateral uniformity and to create niches. In the monastic dining room the table is wenge wood made by Artigiana Legno in Ravenna. Chairs are from Modénature and lamps by Santa & Cole.

LEFT The grace of the house comes from the simplicity of design so the sweeping vaulted ceilings can hold court. The color claret, with its monastic echo, punctuates a predominantly neutral palette.

PLAN Geometric vaulting might be expected to impose a rigid structure on the interior, but the architect has managed to create a thoroughly fluid space. Sightlines, aided by the materials and continuous horizontal planes, run throughout.

FAR LEFT The view over worked land is splendid and romantic. Vineyards (the view from the house) cover 77,500 acres (31,360ha) of Le Marche and registered DOC plots total 25,000 acres (10,120ha).

CENTER LEFT The staircase found its footing very easily—looks very simply inserted—and is distinguished by its contemporary materials, molded from resin and gray marble powder.

LEFT Modern materials (wenge wood, brushed metal, waxed concrete) are a counterbalance to the ancient pitted red brick. There is little ornamentation, often the case in houses built for a warm climate, not so much for security reasons (many people rent their homes seasonally), but because bric-a-brac has little place in a venue for relaxation.

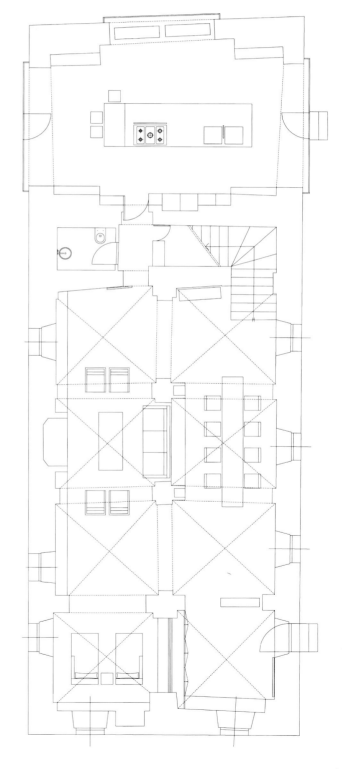

waterside

Living by water brings on the whole fewer challenges than other types of terrain. Nature is on your side, much of the essentials for life at your doorstep. The only major hazard is the risk of flooding (or occasionally, heaven forbid, a tsunami or tidal wave); hence it is of course crucial not to build too close to the water, unless the land is markedly above water level.

In most respects, however, having water nearby makes living in a hot climate much easier. Provision of utilities is rarely a problem: not only is there a supply of water, but usually such areas are relatively inhabited, even built-up, and have basic amenities laid on. And if they don't, even if there is no road, access by water may be an option. The very reason humans first lived by water was for transportation.

Water also makes hot climates more liveable, cooler. In itself it tends to ameliorate extremes of temperature on nearby land, since water heats up and cools down more slowly than land. This means that land alongside water will always have a milder climate than that in the center of a land mass. Even a river or lake has this effect to a certain extent, although not as markedly as an ocean. And the water is always there for a quick cooling dip.

If the sea contains a cold current, a mass of water flowing from temperate or polar regions toward the equator, then its cooling effect on nearby coastal land and air will be even greater. The major such cooling currents in the world's oceans are those flowing south down the coast of California (and to a lesser extent that of Portugal) and north up the west coasts of South America, southern Africa, and western Australia.

Breezes are another characteristic of watersides. On a hot day, as air over the land heats up, it rises, drawing in cooler, damper air from over the sea—a sea breeze. At night or in winter, the air over the sea may become cooler than that over the land, so it in turn rises, drawing air from the land out to sea in the form of a land breeze. These effects also occur, to a lesser extent, by lakesides, and for anyone living near the water in a hot climate, they provide blessed relief. If coastal land is hilly, winds off the sea (be they local sea breezes or regional prevailing winds) may bring rain, too, as the incoming air rises over the hills and cools, so that any water it is carrying condenses and forms precipitation.

Whether or not your waterside property benefits from breezes, even the vision of water or the sound of it can seem cooling. At the house built by Seth Stein at Plettenberg Bay, on the southern coast of South Africa, the breeze is a wake-up call, a delightful tonic when it comes, but the mere sight of the wide, open bay where dolphins and seals gambol can expand the senses. The riverside property in southwestern France is an altogether different experience, a soothing relaxant and escape from the pressures of urban life. This terrain may be easier, but it is not challenge-free.

Building by water requires certain types of materials, which will not rot despite the damp and perhaps salt. A wooden house may seem particularly appropriate by the sea, but it will look very different a couple of years after being built, and even hardwoods may not survive well. Any house by the sea will need more attention to upkeep because of the weathering.

Visually, too, there are specific considerations. Light is reflected more by water than by land, and this must be taken into account in positioning and sizing windows. White or concrete buildings may be appropriate, partly to reflect the sun and avoid absorbing heat and partly for their visual freshness.

OPPOSITE The River Lot rises at Mont Lozère in the Cévennes mountain region. As it approaches the point where it joins the Garonne, it slows down and meanders its way through scenic countryside where we find a magnificent barn conversion.

Pour les prunes!

Pour les prunes! For a barn conversion in southwestern France, backing onto the gentle reaches of the River Lot, the local architects aimed "to conserve a pre-existing ambience, to play with materials and volumes on location to establish continuity between the ancient barn and the new abode."

There is a blessed little corner of southwestern France, on the Atlantic side, made up of gently rolling hills, fields of corn and sunflowers, winding roads empty of cars, and pretty towns and villages, where people always have time to talk. Lot-et-Garonne is named after the Lot and Garonne rivers; currently part of the Aquitaine region, it is one of the 83 *départements* first created at the end of the French Revolution in 1789 from parts of Guyenne and Gascogne.

Agriculture not only prospers here, its produce is famous throughout France: cereals such as maize are grown, cattle are raised and dairy farming practiced. Fruit growing is a specialty, notably plums, strawberries, tomatoes, nuts and melons. The plums, used for making the famous Agen prunes, bear no resemblance to the kind served up for school lunches. Rather they are exotic affairs based on a graft (*prune d'ente*). The "date-plum" (which describes it best) was probably brought back from the Middle East by crusaders. Dried by a special process, it is delicious in many local recipes.

This barn, or *grange* in French (so much more wistful), like many in the region, had two earlier identities: for keeping animals, in this case cattle, and for drying plums. It was scooped up by a smart Parisian lady, originally from this region, as a rural second home near to family and friends, but for regular use, not just summer dwelling: the region has a temperate climate, dominated by the Atlantic, with mild winters and long spring and fall (summers can be very hot, and drier than neighboring Dordogne). Having seen their award-winning work in a French magazine, she called in Bordeaux architects Olivier Martin and Virginie Gravière, a young married couple.

Since the area is swamped with agricultural factories, they thought it appropriate to use fundamental materials in the build: "From the first visit our aim was to convince the client not to destroy the brutal beauty of the building,"

TOP The barn's orientation to the River Lot meant the creation of a window wall, a 20ft-(6m-) tall façade of glass 52ft (16m) wide, which rises upward on its steel frame. The elegantly curving upper canopy is plywood.

ABOVE The husband-and-wife architect team took a rustic barn with soul up a notch or two. The riverside effect is of a glass cathedral. Floors inside are polished concrete. This is plum country; the barn was used for plum drying.

RIGHT Architects Olivier Martin and Virginie Gravière say the remit was to "domesticate the space without removing its brute force." The outline of the old hay storeroom has delineated the spacious open-plan living room.

RIGHT "For the barn—its *mise en scène*—the river is nothing less than inspiring and glorious," say the architects.

FAR RIGHT On the opposite façade to the window wall, small original openings help bring air into the interior.

FAR RIGHT, BELOW Inside walls exhibit rusticity, floors modernity. "The client was married to the concept. It was a very humane adventure," say the architects.

says Martin. Once they had emptied the space, they set about producing a platform upon which to play with a multiplicity of materials.

The other issue was to establish a clear link with the river without disturbing the composition of the farm. "Without touching its exterior, we looked to install a scene for living, totally committed to contemplation of the river that flows at its foot." Thus the architects took the gabled wall facing the river and completely opened it up. "The entire distribution of interior space was to serve this exclusive liaison with the water."

Inside, solid walls made from an assemblage of flat terracotta bricks and stone typify the meshing seen locally. The barn's proportions equally echo local tradition: two side walls are extremely short, with the roof aiming high. The 4,000sq ft (400sq m) footprint is assisted by the two low walls since it would be very awkward as a home if the overall volume were so great. This way the effect is more cathedral, less museum.

In the kitchen area, walls are original and traditional—stone and brick in horizontal layers. A farmhouse table sits alongside colorful 1950s chairs and stools of unknown provenance, adding a stylish but personal 1950s and '60s feel. The presence of stainless steel and concrete (floors throughout are polished concrete) imposes a radical element on homespun materials.

The blend is true to the original barn and its environs. Such conversions can be daunting, but perhaps less so when a large, gentle river sets the tone.

LEFT Plywood, concrete, and cement are used liberally throughout the private quarters, staircase, and bedrooms, and dominate the scheme, resulting in a simple vocabulary and homogenous build. Although modernized to contemporary standards, the barn still displays much of its original DNA, as in the splendid beams.

SKETCHES The architects' sketches show the two façades in plan, the back fitting in with the countryside and the brand-new glass front with its dramatic personality.

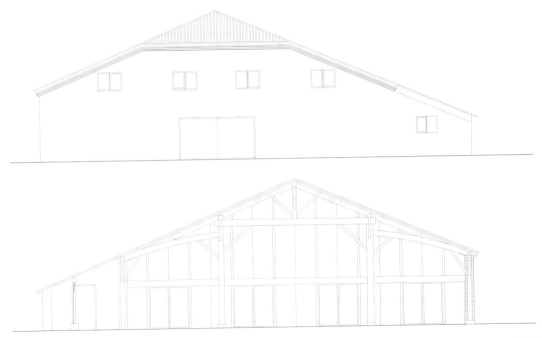

Cape escape

By the wide, sandy South African beach at Plettenberg Bay, overlooking the balmy Indian Ocean near where it meets the Atlantic, London-based architect Seth Stein has built a rather romantic yet modern beach house for clients Lucille and Richard Lewin, who were formerly deeply immersed in the UK'S fashion industry.

The house takes the form of two shoeboxes, one "floating," cantilevered and twisted, on top of the other, held in place, or rather space, by *pilotis* or posts. The rear is dominated by a plain façade of windowless wall; this is true Seth Stein, who enjoys stark concrete—although more reductivist than brutalist—and the odd shadow gap. His main challenge was to build a house that screened its extremely close neighbors from view (in this area land is premium, plots surprisingly small); he managed to obscure the neighbors without obscuring a single view, for anyone.

The front of the house, the beach side (the beach is a short stroll over the dunes), is a complete surprise and rather humanizing. In a city, the house might have looked good all white, but here it needed to merge with the surroundings. The rugged *fynbos*, flowing bushes and grasses that pervade the region, are in abundance. "We wanted the garden to come right up to the house," says the architect, who cites the area as Africa's Hamptons, "with better views." The rolling dunes and pale beaches of South Africa's Eastern and Western Cape provinces are fast becoming a seasonal

OPPOSITE The upper floor of bedrooms is enclosed behind *latte* eucalyptus sunscreens that can be opened with a counterweight mechanism to offer uninterrupted views of the ocean. They are backed by conventional glazing in sliding panels.

THIS PAGE The ground floor opens up completely to views of the Robberg nature reserve. The clean white living area, almost an outdoor room, gives onto the eucalyptus-lined terrace with its niche seating.

destination for Europeans, an influx that is without question influencing local architecture, new villas springing up all over.

From here, the views are across the water to the Robberg nature reserve, an uninhabited peninsula "very good for an afternoon hike," according to owner Richard Lewin. The seascape itself is stunning, the bay teaming with wildlife—seals, sharks, and whales are frequently spotted in a smorgasbord of fish activity (quite literally: the sharks hunt seals, the seals hunt sardines). Interestingly, local fish cannot cross from the waters of the Indian Ocean to those of the Atlantic, due to the dramatic temperature change.

The most delightful part of the house is its wall siding of *latte* eucalyptus. This is made of untreated eucalyptus poles bound to a frame with finely worked copper wire, and is traditionally used for fences and stock barriers in this part of the Cape. Five years after it was built, the copper has begun to oxidize and stain the wood. Eucalypts are Australian trees, but are now so much part of the South African flora (not itself rich in trees that produce useful timber) that their wood is not expensive, and it has the great advantage of being so naturally full of aromatics that it repels both fungi and insects. It is very long-lasting and can be exposed to the weather without special treatment.

The latte screens provide an extraordinary quality of light, a striated luminance that animates the spaces into overgrown sundials, the slits of light moving as the day progresses. The effect is reminiscent of the porch of Alvar Aalto's Villa Mairea in Finland, where wood poles celebrate the forest from which they were cut, as well as offering a welcome homeliness. Stein needed to add a human quality to his clients' home to counteract the otherwise crisp starkness.

The ground floor of the house is completely open plan, except for a small maid's kitchen and toilet facilities. Upstairs a 75ft (23m) corridor running the length of the house, glazed at both ends with a long skylight overhead, gives onto four bedrooms that all face the sea.

According to Stein, the project was not blighted by building laws: almost any design would be accepted as long as the house was under a certain height: "It is a fantastic place to build," he says, "with few restrictions." The quality of local workmanship meant details could be worked finely by hand, achieving a standard of craft and finish rare in Europe for cost reasons.

The couple bought the site to create the ultimate vacation retreat with Stein, who had "otherwise designed" their lives (working on their London townhouse and flagship Whistles stores). He generally takes a modern, minimal approach, projects ranging from a tiny Finnish island to a Lutyens building in London's Pall Mall. This house has become a turning-point for him and a new benchmark in quality beach housing.

PLAN The house has a tilted axis within the footprint of the site. Its *pilotis* (columns) suggest that it can pivot.

OPPOSITE The pool is cleverly orientated, shielded from harsh sun by a wall that also obscures the neighbors' house. Another wall channels a waterfall into the pool: the peaceful sound of falling water is omnipresent.

ABOVE LEFT The living room, incorporating kitchen and dining, is completely open to the side terraces, sheer curtaining softening the light. Here, too, Stein used simple but contrasting, slightly textured materials.

ABOVE The rear is dominated by a floating rendered façade on the first floor, the whole upper section appearing to be supported by *pilotis*. The double garage is integral to the house, which is crowned by a huge roof terrace with an open-air shower.

LEFT Where possible, inside and out, furniture is rendered as a structural element. External floating walls are Barragan-esque but, unlike the color-oriented Mexican architect, Stein has a tonal approach in his use of neutral shades. Stand-alone objects are African and statuesque.

Tasman tranquility
Nestling on the far southern coast of Australia at Merimbula, overlooking the sparkling Tasman Sea, is a striking timber and concrete family home. "Green" in many ways, it is also, according to its architect Clinton Murray, a classic, "a homage to the 1970s Australian beach house."

The southern coast of New South Wales has a temperate climate, avoiding the extreme climate patterns prevalent in other coastal regions of Australia (and is thus less hot than many of the other locations featured in this book). Merimbula lies on a stretch known as the Sapphire Coast, almost midway between Melbourne and Sydney (around seven hours' drive from either city) on the scenic coastal highway route. Named for its sparkling greenish-blue sea, the far-reaching Tasman, this coast is a haven for whale watching, its inland backdrop an almost continuous thread of state forests and national parks.

On Merimbula's Long Point headland, facing south where the edge of the land just falls away toward an extraordinary view, is a house designed by Clinton Murray for a young family relocating from Canberra. The design was inspired in part by the nearby Wharf house, a 1970s beauty with an exposed structural timber frame. "As with that house, this one holds tight to the ground while allowing you to face the weather and the view head-on," says the architect, who builds exclusively (for the time being at least) residential projects.

The family had found a site they liked but a home on it that did not really suit their needs. Brave enough to start from scratch to achieve the seachange they wanted, they engaged Murray to demolish one residence and create their Tasman House. Murray works with an understanding of the enduring characteristics of carefully chosen materials, such as concrete floors that absorb heat, store it, and let it out gradually; along with his sense of orientation, such elements appealed to the responsible young couple. He likes to build with wood, too. For an award-winning 1997 house also in Merimbula, he used hefty posts and beams recycled from a bridge in rural Victoria.

ABOVE The pool, central to the building's design, stretches out toward the sapphire Tasman Sea.

RIGHT Views are magnificent from every part of this homage to a 1970s beach house.

RIGHT, ABOVE Furniture and accouterments are kept to a minimum, clean and simple. Clutter can be the enemy in a warm climate, and fabric stifling. Louvered doors, a nod to the 1970s, are now back in vogue.

ABOVE Clinton Murray's "green" awareness has meant his signatures generally include excellent orientation and cross-ventilation (no air conditioning), as well as energy-efficient concrete floors that function as thermal mass, conserving heat. Here you can see right through the house.

LEFT The back of the house, or rather the approach, has been landscaped into the hillside. The woodenness of the building is most evident here: its siding will change with time, and some wood weathers beautifully. Clinton, who believes in hands-on involvement, worked closely with his group of three carpenters.

Murray, who has been described in the Australian press as "intense and irreverent," is a likeable fellow, and there is something about this Australian architect's work that falls into similar vein to that of the cherished American architect Charles Gwathmey. Since I am extremely fond of the smaller projects Gwathmey presented in the 1960s and 1970s—the wooden Cubist house built for his parents in Amagansett on Long Island in particular—I am not really surprised I find Clinton Murray's new build here in Merimbula appealing.

For the Tasman House, Murray anchored the L-shaped home around the pool and deck, central to the main wing of the house facing the sea. To the rear of the house, which inclines upward onto a hill to the north, is a garage. From this, you enter the house from the rear through an entry court and immediately have the southerly view over the Tasman Sea. This is the upper level, where guest rooms and a study make up the corner of the building; to the east, beyond the central deck, there is an open-plan living-dining room and, further toward the end of the house, a kitchen.

Downstairs, accessible from a central staircase, the footprint of the house is much the same, anchored by the deck at this level and the over-lengthy pool spilling out toward the sea. Of the sea the architect says, "You can almost fall into it—or dive into the pool." Beneath the garage are storerooms, while at the corner of the building on this lower level are the three children's bedrooms built in strict uniformity (three in a row) and their trapezoid-shaped playroom. The master-bedroom suite is directly underneath the living and dining room at the eastern end of the house.

Ostensibly a wooden structure with vast windows front and back, the house is made breezy by louvered glass window panels—possibly its most 1970s inflection. It was built with a team of three carpenters, Ty Simpson, David Gardener, and Don O'Connell, with Alan Simpson heading up the building team. The landscaping is by Clinton's brother Andrew Murray.

Gwathmey's work has been described, by the great architect Robert A. M. Stern, as rising "from vernacular roots to the lyricism of high art" and "liberated from the constraints of the prevailing modernism." I believe Clinton Murray's work will similarly continue to impress for its rigor and its clarity, for its movement away from current tastes and for the fact that he builds in response to human functions and dimensions, with respect for economy of means.

ABOVE Inside, sliding doors help to reapportion the rooms. The interior space has a seamless flow despite the fact that there are many functional elements to the house, home to a family with three children. Ease and efficiency was a must.

BELOW & BELOW RIGHT Murray anchored the house around the pool and deck, which are central to the main wing of the building, facing the sea (the house forms an L shape). When you are in the pool, you can swim right into the belly of the structure.

ABOVE At the western corner of the building on the lower level are the three regimented children's bedrooms and their trapezoid-shaped playroom. Above them are guest rooms and study. The house is a permanent home, not a vacation extravaganza. It is inhabited all year round.

ABOVE RIGHT This end of the building houses the living-dining room on the upper level and, beneath it, the master-bedroom suite.

PLAN The L-shaped house is clearly defined by the floor plan (here showing the lower level), with the pool jutting out perpendicular to the principal wing. The landscaping was very relevant to the position of the build, although the view and sea orientation took precedence over all aspects in the final plan.

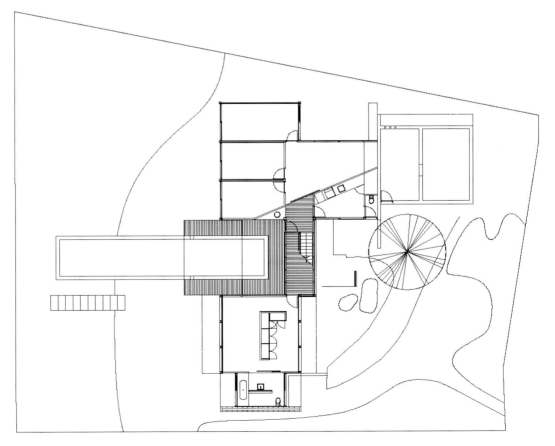

hillside

Living on a hill is akin to sitting in a tall-backed chair. It makes you feel more important—as if you are at the top of your ladder, so to speak. As Alfred, Lord Tennyson wrote, "Live and Lie reclined on the hills like Gods together, careless of mankind. For they lie beside their nectar and the bolts are hurled far below them in the valleys, and the clouds are lightly curled round their golden houses, girdled with the gleaming world."

Besides any psychological advantage, living on a hill brings its own climatic benefits. For accurate assessment of climate, several factors that influence temperature and precipitation must be taken into account: not only the obvious question of latitude—which determines the angle of the sun's rays and hence the intensity of solar energy received—but also variables such as elevation (alternatively referred to as altitude), prevailing wind direction, and topography. Elevation is the height above sea level. As you go higher up a mountain, the air pressure decreases and its molecules spread farther and farther apart. Less dense air is cooler than dense air, so the farther above sea level you are, the lower the temperature will be.

Furthermore, being on a hill generally means you are exposed to flowing air, with all the cooling benefits a breeze can bring in a hot climate. The precise impact will depend on whether you are on the windward or leeward side of the hill in terms of prevailing winds, and on details of local topography, which will serve to channel airflow. These issues must be thoroughly considered when siting and orientating a building. The Southern African house revealed in this chapter was built atop a hill overlooking a lake; it is hot up there, but the cool breeze even makes it conceivable to play tennis—at least at certain times of the day.

Less dense air can hold less water, so as air rises over mountains it deposits any excess water molecules it is carrying as rain or snow (or snow, in conditions where the temperature is cold enough). If the prevailing winds bring air that has just traveled over water, it will be carrying a great deal of moisture, which will fall on the windward side of the mountains; by the time the air reaches the leeward side, it will be largely rained out, and the leeward side will be left in a rain shadow, much drier—another factor to consider in choosing a site.

Shade is also an issue. Being on a hot hilltop brings the risk of over-exposure to the sun, but if you use the shading of the hill well, choosing the right side and taking advantage of natural irregularities, you can make the topography work in your favor. Again, this requires careful planning, just as the legendary 20th-century designer Eileen Gray spent a year viewing her plot at Roquebrune in the south of France from all angles and in all weathers and moods before building there.

Building on a hill must be clever, perhaps curving around the hillside or creating intricate shapes that allow three-dimensional movement up and down as well as to and fro within the building as conditions of sun and wind change according to the time of day or night. The Ibiza house featured in this chapter is closed on one side and opens up to the sea on the other, thereby directing its use.

A further challenge is simply to transport the necessary materials up to the site. In the case of an ambitious project, it can literally take years to complete a building. But, as all three of these examples show, it is worth it simply for the impact of the site, the views, the sense of living like a god.

OPPOSITE The predominantly glass house designed by Helena Arahuete of Lautner Associates is located on the South Sister of the Twin Sisters in Napa, California, with an elevation of 2,259ft (689m). Views are magnificent.

Hilltop eyrie

Perched on a Napa hilltop above the vineyards, this superlative example of California architecture, with its window walls and magnificent views, brings together birdlike grace and sophisticated engineering. This is what living on top of the world is about: using 21st-century skills to make the most of an elevated location and create a home where you can really breathe.

Up until now I have held close to my heart the house I think is one of the most spectacular in the world. It was for sale again at the very end of the 20th century for an awful lot of money, and I could only dream of owning it. The architect, the late John Lautner, designed (with an interior by someone else whose work I admire wholeheartedly, the late Michael Taylor) a magnificent oceanfront house on a rocky promontory at La Chuza Point in Malibu, its baying glass windows giving view to rough waters beneath. The interior incorporated natural elements—huge riverbed boulders, for example, to break up the geometry of the architecture inside, as well as Taylor's fantastic scheme of spherical white

ABOVE Sloping roofs, high from the outside but low on the interior courtyard side, capture the vistas and visually pull them toward the house. Angular rooflines echo the forms of the distant mountains. The upper level is 90 percent glass in 15ft (4.5m) panels.

BELOW On the south side is a 50ft (15m) indoor/outdoor lap pool. Two glass panels over it slide aside on motorized overhead tracks. Its supporting beam tapers, lessening the apparent heftiness with a grace typical of the architect. Chairs are Summit.

The decks are slate-covered in Lautner style; concrete and slate stairs lead to the entrance. The combination of materials—fir, mahogany (inside), concrete and glass—makes for a truly harmonious vision at one with the surroundings.

ABOVE In the center of the house is the two-story courtyard. Despite being surrounded by 1,700 acres (688ha) of wooded landscape, the couple decided to contain their own portion of the outdoors within the six-sided house. The courtyard remains cool.

ABOVE RIGHT : Ceilings are paneled in vertical-grain Douglas fir and pitch and sweep, dipping down to 7ft (2m) over built-in sofas, rising to 15ft (4.5m) at the tallest windows. The interior design was aided by Siobhan Brennan of John Wheatman & Associates.

cushions and oversized puffy white sofas. It symbolizes utterly the California dream. Built in 1983, the floors are slabs of slate in almost free form: Lautner had held firm the naturalistic ideals of his teacher, the great Frank Lloyd Wright, but had developed a style all of his own, using glass instead of brick, and local slates and stone.

So when Helena Arahuete, who had worked with Lautner from 1971 until his death in 1994, continued to practice using the Lautner name, I have to say I was a little sceptical and doubted that anything quite as magnificent could ever be created in the name of Lautner again.

I was wrong. This project, completed in 2004 (it was first conceived of in 1998) by Arahuete with Lautner Associates for client John Roscoe, is a superlative example of fine California architecture with its window walls and magnificent views, and quite evidently continues the spirit of Lautner without being pastiche. The Roscoe residence, in Napa, positioned at the very apex of the hill, looks as if it is about to take off, yet is not at odds with the vineyard surroundings. It is splendid on approach and splendid within, and has a grace I have not seen in residential architecture in years. As with the old Lautner, there has to be one amazing fanfare moment and here it is the pool, which transgresses from house to exterior so you can actually swim from inside to out. When the windows slide over at night, or when there is cooler weather, it is possible to swim underneath the glass: a remarkable building feat, and moreover a good idea.

A home's surroundings always pitch the house itself, or should do, and this residence is surrounded by a panorama of sky. Glass houses have often beguiled architects: glass is solid yet invisible, present yet transparent. What Arahuete has done is to create an Expressionistic vision, with what appear to be vast shards of glass exploding into the air. The house gives

ABOVE Arahuete has created her own signature detail in the *faux bois* concrete design on some interior walls. The owners insisted that all fireplaces should be at floor level, no raised hearths.

RIGHT The pool enters the house near breakfast and dining areas separated by a fireplace. The house is composed of expansive spaces, with unobstructed views from every room on the main floor.

views stretching from San Francisco's Golden Gate Bridge on one horizon to the Sierra Nevada on the other. The hills of Napa's wine country roll beneath.

Owners John and Marilyn Roscoe loved hiking in these hills, so they slowly purchased adjoining parcels of land, gathering 1,700 acres (688ha) including two sugar-loaf peaks, the Twin Sisters, that command the immediate area. Roscoe's remit was to give everything to the 360-degree view, and Belgian-born Arahuete, who was raised in Argentina, another country with big landscape, produced unobstructed views from every room on the main floor; even from the kitchen the vista is filled with the Twin Sister peak to the north. As Arahuete says, "The views are a constant presence."

The structure is stern: built of concrete poured in place, it has a steel-beam roof, yet its main floor seems to float lithely above the ground, while its terraces jut out into space. The geometry, stylistically speaking, is not as complicated as it first seems and, despite its angles and the fact that "the perspective of each angle changes as you move," as the architect points out, it cannot be dubbed "de-constructed" as could the more complicated architecture fad of the moment (think Daniel Libeskind and Zaha Hadid). Construction was, however, challenging, and Arahuete was assisted for some elements—for example the pool, which cantilevers over the sloping hillside despite its weight—by Andrew Nasser, the engineer who structured some of Lautner's most challenging designs.

The house, 13,500sq ft (1,254sq m) of interior floor space, has intimate and grander moments, and privacy is still possible within (glass houses have been criticized nonstop for their goldfish-bowl characteristics), not just because of the remoteness of the location, but also thanks to the design. This is achieved even when there are guests, as there often are, once three hundred at once. The main space consists of kitchen and dining, living and pool rooms. "We all have simple needs, really," says Roscoe. Downstairs, sunk into the hillside a little, are a library, utility rooms, exercise rooms, and two guest rooms.

As Lautner learned from Frank Lloyd Wright, Arahuete has learned from John Lautner. A magnificent 21st-century *oeuvre* has already been built. In John Roscoe's words, "We are very pleased with the house designed by Helena Arahuete and very pleased with the house that has been constructed. We realize and appreciate the great effort expended by those who strove valiantly to overcome the difficulties inherent in the project."

LEFT With all its wood, the house has a fire-retardent metal roof. A prerequisite was to be able to cool it down to 72°F (23°C) on hot days, but nights can be cold.

TOP The kitchen has been kept to a minimum, functional and slick. Slate floors throughout give visual continuity.

ABOVE Exterior steps lead from upper floor to lower within the courtyard. This house is far from sedentary, with numerous passageways.

PLAN The massive interior space of 13,500sq ft (1,254sq m) has a steel-beamed roof. The plan of the house shows its originality and ingenuity.

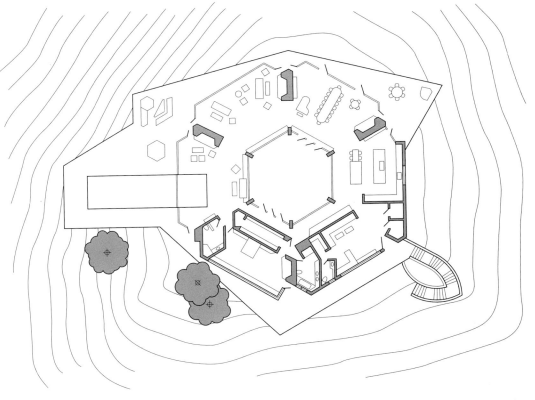

Little boxes on the hillside
Casa Na Xemena, the house built by architect Ramón Esteve in the remote landscape of the hamlet of Na Xemena for client José Gandia, takes prime place on Ibiza's glorious craggy north coast and looks out upon absolute nothingness but sea and sky horizon: the house is silent.

Enclosed at the rear, the south side, the house remains as cool as a cucumber despite the raging sun, which, at times in the Balearics, seems unstoppable. As a teenager I vacationed in the Balearics on occasion and thinking back, I believe the reason we imagine the climate is really hot is because we go there to vacation. In Marrakech, where the outside temperature is hotter, and the arid desert dust drifts into our lungs, the fact that the city is a working hub makes the heat seem more palatable. In Cairo and Giza, too, the climate can be almost too much at times, but we cope with it because we are busy sightseeing and thus perhaps equip ourselves better. Ibiza, on the other hand, has no business, just relaxation, and that is when we feel it the most: up for a swim, a light breakfast, a book by the pool, lunch, and finally a sundowner on the terrace—it is all about the heat and, quite frankly, we soak it up it, as long as we can find refuge inside.

Originally one small, boxlike *finca* or cottage, Casa Na Xemena has been extended to a veritable *enfilade* of *finca*s, all open-plan inside and linked together with little interior upset except for the odd floor-level change. The house belongs to José Gandia of Gandia Blasco, a Spanish furniture firm that dates back to the 1940s and is best known for its outdoor and lighting products. It is his second home and he rarely comes alone: guest rooms are abundant, six with *en suite* bathrooms, and room for more. The guest suites are molded into the form of the house under the main level so it is difficult to see them from either front or back.

BELOW Casa Na Xemena, high on the craggy north coast of Ibiza, is a spectacular example of coherent and sequential design: from the rear the boxes comprising the house appear uniform, but the sea-facing view gives an understanding of the many levels.

RIGHT The infinity pool has been designed to run along two axes, across the front of the *enfilade* of boxlike forms, and then to stretch out towards the Mediterranean on the north side of the island.

FAR LEFT Bathed in light, the white building pays homage to the domestic architecture of the Balearics. From the rear, Moorish undertones are evident, quite a common sight in many Spanish regions. A common finish, white reflects both light and heat.

LEFT The architect has added many refuges from the elements such as terraces that fall into semi-shade at certain times of day according to the position of the sun in the sky. Rigid overhead sunshades are permanent and static.

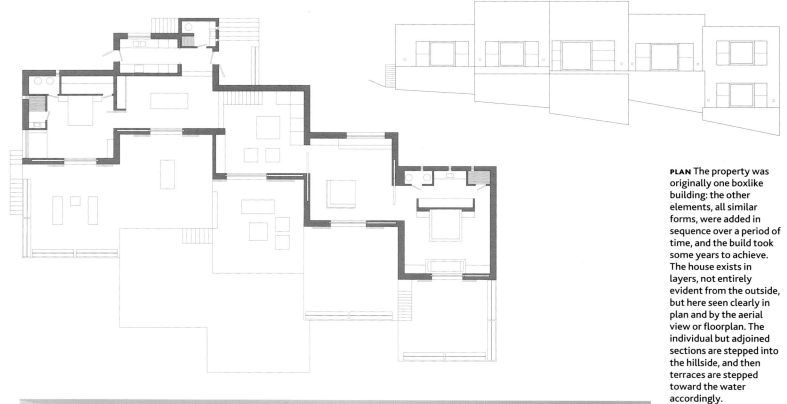

PLAN The property was originally one boxlike building: the other elements, all similar forms, were added in sequence over a period of time, and the build took some years to achieve. The house exists in layers, not entirely evident from the outside, but here seen clearly in plan and by the aerial view or floorplan. The individual but adjoined sections are stepped into the hillside, and then terraces are stepped toward the water accordingly.

LEFT Iroko wood frames a huge picture window in a bedroom. Outdoor and indoor furniture was made specially for the house by Esteve, but is now available though the owner's furniture firm. Sunken and raised bathtubs in bedroom suites differ in size and form, but are on the whole concrete.

RIGHT A shaft of light from an oblong window hits cantilevered stairs made from iroko wood, and is echoed by a suspended light. Seating is inbuilt and covered in muslin for cool comfort.

LEFT The cobalt blue of the dining room helps delineate the rest of the white space. A bedroom and bathroom at the top of these stairs are encased in a wooden box. Entry to the house is into the dining room (via the steps seen here against the blue wall).

TOP The window in this bathroom area is a slit between two solid gray structures, the bath sunken. Grayness and texture separate the area from the bedroom, although it is very much within the room.

ABOVE A couple of steps help the "layering" of a simple building and add contemporary character. Iroko is used for ceilings and staircase as well as the kitchen, a minute space that indicates barbecues are the norm.

ABOVE RIGHT The bedroom in the wooden box has a low ceiling and is almost clinical in its simplicity. In a warm environment clutter can be stifling. Resin floors are durable, soft to touch, not too cold and easy to clean. Bedding is cotton or linen.

The front, the sea side, facing north away from the sun, is completely open, box-by-box, its infinity pool and terrace just edging onto the rocky hillside and the view beneath. The hill certainly invites a breeze onto the terrace and directly into the house, so much so that hanging lampshades swing gently just to remind us there is some kind of activity out there, life is not extinct. From the other sides, a spattering of small square and oblong perforations in the structure create theatrical lights inside the house by day, and at night beam spots of warm light onto the terrace outside.

Inside, powdery white and cobalt- and indigo-blue-pigmented walls create a thread running through the home, as do floors in gray tones, in almost Cubist manner. Iroko wood, an African hardwood also called Nigerian teak, which is hard and durable in humid climates, is used throughout, for ceilings and staircase as well as the kitchen (whose tiny size suggests that most cooking takes place outdoors). Iroko also frames three huge picture windows—reminiscent of the Groupe 7 house on Capri, also on a rocky coast overlooking water—giving dramatic sea views. Moving from box to box inside the house is seamless and the openings vast: there are no interior doors between the five elements.

The house has been an ongoing project for six years; the final two cube buildings have just been added to the three built in succession before. Somewhat removed from a formally planned geometric scheme, the slow pace of building has resulted in a collection of spaces that is articulated with a natural grace only time can bring.

When the house project began, Gandia Blasco was selling only textiles, but the building of Na Xemena encouraged a furniture collection. "The house dictated the pieces," says architect Esteve from his studio in Valencia. "The building was asking for furniture that was not on the market." The pieces, a neutral style of furniture that can adapt to many settings, have become a staple part of the firm.

Ramón Esteve graduated from the Architecture Superior Technique School of Madrid in 1990 and founded his own studio, realizing several works in Spain from houses to larger commercial projects. Working also in interior and industrial design, he has received prizes for furniture, some of it for Gandia Blasco. Despite the kudos this house has given him, Esteve plans to continue designing commercially, in part because he doesn't like the tendency to make a statement with each individual work. He likes, in every sense, to just blend in.

The architect describes this house as "simple," since the five concrete cubes exhibit a premeditative linking of the topography, the architectonic set integrating into the landscape as it scales the rocky cliff. As he points out, "The main characteristic of the home is its isolation." This is highlighted by the cube form and the metal-framed sunshade, which seems to give the house a border.

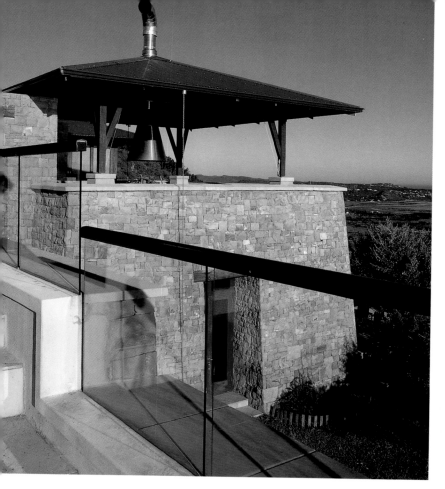

View House

"We created a hilltop bastion-type sandstone structure, growing out of the prehistoric dune and topped with a wide-brimmed floating roof," says architect Johann Slee of his achievement. View House is a vacation home on the picturesque south coast of South Africa, a project where just sandstone, glass, and wood have been used to create a very specific atmosphere; the house is at once peaceful and majestic, monastic yet suitable for a party.

On the top of a hill in Sedgefield, near Knysna, on the coastal road toward Plettenberg Bay, the client—from Holland—bought one of the most breathtaking views in the country and commissioned Slee to build him a vacation compound for his family, who are scattered around the globe. The site, unparalleled in beauty over any location I have set eyes upon (but then I love South Africa), is a prehistoric sand dune overlooking the Swartvlei estuaries.

From the winding hillside approach road, which begins near a rail line and ends what seems miles away at the pinnacle, the fortress looms large, apparently on the very edge of the hill. Despite the natural flora surrounding the house, there is still a rather large private garden (tennis courts, too, but these are to be avoided in midday sun); the approach is through the garden and entry is from the rear.

Enormous double reclaimed doors lead to a monastic interior courtyard which contains a square pond with simple drip fountain. It is used for quiet reflection and meditation, and there is only a wooden bench as furniture, plus one or two enormous pots. "Our architectural palette has its origins in the earth—muted earth colors, textured finishes reflecting abundant sunlight. Our built structures reflect simplicity and honesty, echoing the vernacular of local built forms. The beauty of detail is in the crude simplicity," says the architect.

The structure and its courts give refuge from the harsh elements, but also open up to allow enjoyment of the exterior spaces and spectacular views in panorama. Through the doors opposite the initial entrance is the large rectangular "great hall," not unlike a medieval banqueting hall, which leads out to the terrace and the swimming pool, the latter overhanging the water. Above the swimming pool

TOP LEFT The lo-tech materials used for the fortress-like structure were simply local stone, wood, and glass.

TOP RIGHT From the road beyond the railroad you can see the bastion right at the hill's apex, its roofs alive in the sun.

ABOVE CENTER The four main elements, one on each corner around a courtyard, suggest a medieval castle.

ABOVE On the east viewing platform Slee has built a "floating fire ring" for heat and *braais*, as barbecues are known.

THIS PAGE The disappearing edge pool melts into the lagoon on the west towards the estuary, giving from the main floor of the house. From the front double doors—huge imposing wooden structures—you can see through the courtyard with its meditation pool, into the main hall, not unlike a "great hall" of old, through to the deck and pool. It is one continuum. The upper level of the main floor also falls into a terrace overlooking the estuary.

All bedrooms are interior-designed simply, each one completely differently furnished with local artefacts or *objets trouvés*. No bed is the same as another. Linens and fabrics are generally local although some delightful pieces are European. Floors are stone.

RIGHT This is the inner courtyard, built for contemplation with its serene pool feature.

FAR RIGHT Each bedroom has its own bathroom – almost a prerequisite in a hot climate, bathing being so central to comfort (privacy and escape is another important factor). It does seem very un-Western to bathe with a view, but I think it a great luxury.

PLAN In aerial view the form is clear: public rooms are in the central section with the pool, private at the edges.

on the next level a sun deck has been built, also hanging out from the structure, giving a view over the pool beneath and the estuary and hills beyond.

At all four corners of the principal building stand fortress-like towers, each with a spiral stone staircase leading to quaint bedrooms and minimalist bathrooms. The bedrooms, on ground and upper levels, are individually designed, with unique pieces of African and antique furniture, and both bedrooms and bathrooms have enormous windows giving splendid views at every opportunity. Although the house design can accommodate extremely large family gatherings, these tower bedrooms are a retreat far from the madding crowd.

"We create space to live in. Our expertise lies in residential spaces, vacation homes and lodges, and selective commercial work that falls into our design philosophy," says the architect. Slee & Co is a multidisciplined architecture and design practice with offices in Johannesburg (see pages 40–3 for Slee's own Johannesburg home) and Knysna. Having been an architect since the 1980s, Slee believes "South Africa is alive with possibility" for its room to build and its different vernaculars throughout the vast land—and for the talent, too. "The philosophy behind our design is to incorporate and respect the diverse aspirations and heritages of our

clients; to learn from advanced technologies and to create a vernacular architecture, embracing our unique people, skills, climate, and space," the architect explains.

One of Slee's projects, in his home town of Johannesburg in 2005, won *South African House and Leisure* magazine's "House of the Year" competition, in a country where new building is abundant. His design of the Red House, another recent residential project, was selected as winner in 2004 of the Residential Built Project category in the prestigious Cityscape Architectural Review Awards in Dubai, where all entries came from developing countries and judging criteria were based upon the design's contribution to world architectural culture, invention, imagination, environmental awareness, and appropriateness. Wherever Slee builds in his vast country, he uses indigenous materials and local stone, yet his designs travel well—they could be adapted to suit many hot terrains.

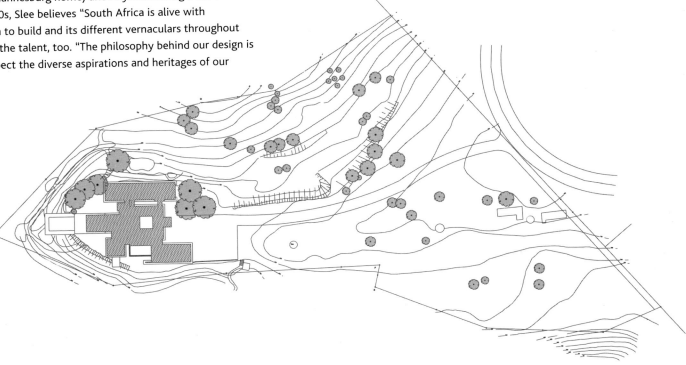

streetside

Cities create their own microclimates. Whatever climatic belt it is in, an urban area will always be a few degrees warmer than its surroundings, thanks to the heat exuded by its buildings and inhabitants, along with the effects of traffic. Buildings absorb the sun's heat by day and give it off at night, as well as generating heat themselves via their heating or cooling systems. They also create local winds, funneling air flows down channels between structures. As a result of such factors, cloud cover and precipitation over cities will usually also differ markedly from surrounding regions. The effect of all this is that—without even starting to take into account the impact of pollution—the climatic problems of hot-climate living are exacerbated in a city.

The other key influence on an urban home is that mostly space is at a premium. This may radically cut back the options for combating the elements—some just do require space in which to spread out—and it will no doubt mean that neighbors are nearby, and even if their homes do not physically block the ideal build, there will at least be psychological, aesthetic, or legislative constraints on architectural expression (although these can serve to stimulate inventiveness).

Orientation, for instance, is a given: you have to face the street. Even if it would better meet light and shade requirements to site the house at an angle, there is rarely the choice—unless you are highly innovative and come up with a clever scheme such as shifting the axis of the building so that it meets all criteria (see pages 108–11). This kind of non-conformist thinking and hard work are required on many counts, to deal with sorting out air flows and cool spots as well as the more standard challenges.

Assuming building permissions and local authorities cannot be negotiated, the result may be a compromise on exterior design and a focus instead on the interior—although not in these examples, where the challenge has been met. A possible approach to urban design is to retain parts of an existing building and add new elements to it—a completely new build is relatively rare in most places—in which case we usually attempt to highlight what is worth preserving historically; in London this tends to mean Georgian, in Chicago or Los Angeles 20th-century. Such principles may seem restrictive, but they can be food for inspiration, too.

In non-urban hot environments, outdoor living is fundamental to coping with the heat, to the extent that divisions between indoor and outdoor often blur. But in a city, spending all day in the garden is frequently unviable: the house may have no garden or other outdoor space, and even if it does, issues of privacy and noise may discourage its use. Shaded balconies and roof terraces, up above prying eyes and the worst of the noise and pollution, and perhaps equipped with simple yet effective wood or rattan-type screens, thus come into their own as outdoor rooms. Similarly, and especially in newly designed homes, huge picture windows may be employed, although these must be carefully thought out so that they fulfill their objective of providing an almost-outdoor room without the noise or pollution, but do not bring the oven effect of a greenhouse or any significant loss of privacy.

Architects working in a city may not be able to let their imaginations soar as they might elsewhere, but they do have to stretch their creative thinking to find solutions to often more complex problems if they are to achieve climate-sensitive urban design and provide people with a comfortable thermal environment. And at least city builds are easier in one respect: amenities are always close at hand.

OPPOSITE The Wrap House in Melbourne, Australia, spearheaded by Simon Knott, is constructed from rendered blockwork on a steel-portal frame and, unconventionally but correctly, faces sideways toward the north so the sun is easily controlled. A 2,400-gallon (9,000-liter) water-storage tank is located in the basement car garage to allow water reticulation to the garden and lawns.

Boxing clever

Wrap House, winner of the Australian Design Awards Interior Design Selection 2004, was built for a semi-retired couple in a rather genteel Melbourne suburb, Toorak, previously better known for its red-tile roofs, brick-veneer siding and disregard for orientation than for modernistic vision.

The house's architects were the firm BKK (Black Kosloff Knott), spearheaded by Simon Knott. All three directors of the firm, founded in 2000, are practicing architects—Tim Black, Julian Kosloff, and Simon Knott—and at least one of them is always closely involved in any project taken on, "to ensure the appropriate placement of resources and to take maximum advantage of the depth of skills" available within the office. Highly academic in their study and execution of their work, the trio claim to be actively involved in the local culture of design (after all, architecture does not happen in a vacuum), annually curating the "Lite" exhibition as part of the worldwide *Faites de la Lumière* celebration of creating light. All have been university educators in both architectural design and technology at RMIT (Royal Melbourne Institute of Technology) and maintain roles

OPPOSITE, TOP The house was sited to minimize excavation and use existing levels. A simple steel portal frame fixed to a suspended concrete slab was infilled with panels of concrete block and timber stud, and rendered over.

OPPOISTE, BOTTOM Environmentally, the house incorporates a number of energy-saving techniques. It was pushed to the southern edge of the site to maximize the northern solar aspect and connect living and external space.

THIS PAGE In the living area, materials were selected on the basis of finish, such as render, laminate, and concrete floors requiring little maintenance. Concrete block and concrete screed floors were utilized for insulation.

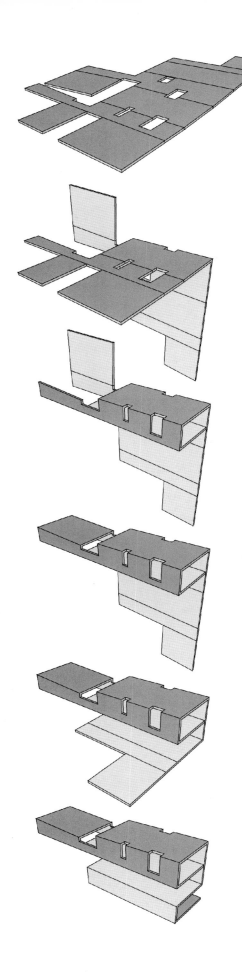

with the Royal Australian Institute of Architects. An award-winning firm, BKK's high-profile design projects have included commercial, institutional, retail, residential, and governmental builds.

This kind of resumé, the scholarly kind, let me tell you as a "veteran" architecture writer (I was not entirely amused by this so-called accolade which appeared in print recently since it makes me sound ancient), is impressive but often makes my eyes roll, and I have to take a deep breath before even beginning to unravel the kind of work such highly esteemed architects are up to. How can I explain without upsetting people? Wholly academic firms, or those who practice from the philosophical standpoint—or those who are too pure in their do-gooding or at least sound as if they are—often produce work that somehow manages to evade the interest of the general public, except for some of the true talents of our times such as Zaha Hadid. Sometimes the work is so "architectural" it is impossible to see its merit without reading the subtext. On occasion only other architects quite see the point. I see a lot of this kind of work at the colleges, where quite frankly I am not surprised they go into such depth of study—after all, it takes longer to qualify as an architect than as a doctor. But in the real world, the holier-than-thou approach can be a little off-putting, "good" as it is meant to be. I am aware that architects have to study long and hard to be able to secure our safety, to study the laws and bylaws of the land, and learn how to build magnificent *oeuvres* while learning about the more fundamental elements such as water-cooling systems and air conditioning, but I am not sure the outside world needs this much information. When I need a doctor, I want a diagnosis and prognosis, and that is about it—no deep discussion about cell counts and hemoglobin levels. Well, with architecture it's the same. How does it look and how does it feel and will it last long, stylistically and otherwise, are my first, and often only, questions.

It is therefore thrilling when looking at and experiencing the work of BKK, particularly the Wrap House in the Melbourne suburbs, that they have, fortunately, simply built a fantastic house. You don't need the subtext to realize how fantastic the house actually is—although it is relevant to know that the firm's design methodology "focuses on a response to both occupant and site, providing a solution that shies away from the merely fashionable aspects of contemporary design," hoorah!

It is true that the architects make much of the notion of wrap, a proposition about how architecture might approach from other directions than customary orientation and structure. It is suggested by BKK that the design for the Wrap House comes from a sequence of folds in a carefully cut flat sheet. In a way, the wrap hardly matters, for here is a series of dramatic domestic spaces light years beyond the imagination of the builders of the surrounding brick-tile mini-mansions. "There is little or no resemblance to the traditional spatiality of a house with long corridors and a sequential layout of rooms. Rather, a progression through the house is highly modulated. Spaces flow from one to the next and are largely differentiated by their height and volume," comments architect Simon Knott. In fact the expression does not seem particularly to relate to the way the rooms are arranged inside, only impacting on the ground-floor library and upper-floor master bedroom, which both have large picture windows exposed to the fierce westerly sun in the afternoons; I imagine the picture windows are there for formal reasons to complete the wrap, and they do have integral sun blinds.

According to the clients, the architects have bestowed upon them everything they wanted; the steep approach from street up to the house's ground-floor level was a given, due to the steeply sloping site, something the architects had to work with and not at all their fault. In the final analysis, this might be "clever" architecture, but it is good architecture and moreover a very sound home.

PLAN The house's flatpack-like flattened plane is folded around internal service blocks, "shaping" the interior space by providing an envelope. The Wrap House presents a number of differentiated and varied volumes.

RIGHT, ABOVE Highlight colors are chosen to add points of reference and draw the interior through to the lush landscaping. The banding to the exterior render is carried though to the internal face by alternating bands of gloss and flat paint.

RIGHT At the upper level, the elevation reads as a series of solid blocks separated by glazing. Large picture windows grace the master bedroom, which faces the street and the fierce afternoon sun. The sun blinds also offer privacy.

FAR RIGHT Concrete block, render, plasterboard, and metal deck are the simple infill materials that complete the fabric of the house. Through economic detailing and selection, the interior fit-out is a cost-effective solution.

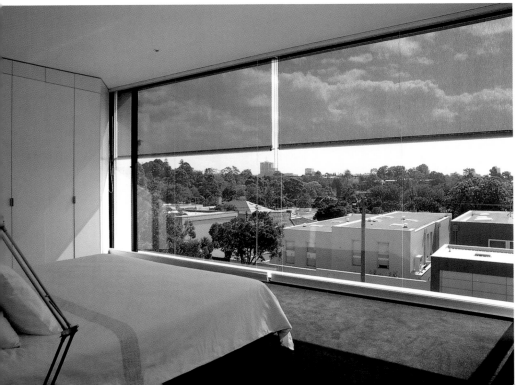

(CASE STUDY)

Fabric of invention

Steven Ehrlich is an urban architect, if ever there was one, for his values and principles. But while he works at the forefront of new technology, he is also influenced by the courtyards and souks of African architecture, especially of Morocco and Nigeria. The results are evident in the verging-on-industrial yet caravanserai-like home he has built for himself and his wife on a narrow corner plot in Venice, Los Angeles.

Ehrlich sees himself as an "architectural anthropologist," understanding connections between "architecture and culture, people and place." Founded in 1979, his award-winning Steven Ehrlich Architects (SEA) is a 20-strong sole proprietorship based in Culver City, California. Here he finds himself happily in the vanguard of technological advancement and the truly modern world with all its lively trappings, and with a little more space to work than architects in the cramped conditions of Cairo or Mexico City, for instance in his "high-tech high-touch" environment, a 13-acre (5.2ha) plot designed for DreamWorks for their one-thousand-strong creative workforce.

Apart from successful designs for lofts in Venice Beach and his pending "Multi-Family" housing project at City Place in Santa Ana, Ehrlich has also

ABOVE LEFT The vista on entry to the house sweeps right through and out the other side. Crazy paving is a quirky addition but right at home in the hustle and bustle that is Venice, LA.

ABOVE To one side of the main living space is a smaller room for television and reading. A modern home need not be a bare home: here books are neatly housed in floor-to-ceiling bookshelves.

RIGHT A 16ft- (5m-) tall window wall slides open to the sculptural trunks of an Aleppo pine tree. This is Ehrlich's creation of courtyard. In the courtyard living room two Boomerang chairs are by Richard Neutra; leather poufs, Moroccan rugs, and even the colors echo the souks of the architect's travels.

sensitively restored some fine modern classics. These have included an addition to Richard Neutra's 1938 Lewin Residence which, cradled at the base of the Santa Monica bluffs, had heard nothing in recent times but the roar of the Pacific Coast Highway. Here, for clients, Ehrlich created a cloistered tripartite environment, each part of it, according to the architect, "lying in conversation with the nuances of the original structure," and most relevantly, he built a wall between the residence and the street as a shield against the traffic beyond, which of course did not exist in 1938 Santa Monica. Urban and suburban housing really does have far more of a fight with the modern world than the rural house has with nature.

With libraries, biotech laboratories, middle schools, and civic centers under his belt, what then do we expect from the home he has built for himself and wife, author Nancy Griffin? The 700 Palms residence addresses the freedoms as well as the constraints of building in Venice, California. "By maximizing volume, light, and privacy on a narrow lot with sensitivity to scale and context, the design presents raw, honest materials appropriate to the grittiness of the Venice environment," says its architect. The house dissolves the barriers between indoor and out, as did Richard Neutra and Rudolph Schindler houses of yesteryear, creating flexible space that takes full advantage of the benign climate. This is realized through use of a wood-and-steel-framed structure of seven limbs that encloses the yard in a roll-down scrim hung on a skeletal steel frame. It is a vision more expected in

OPPOSITE Above the lap pool a steel framework supports orange and yellow fabric shades that move in all directions. I find this combination of true-grit urban living with the poetry of the fabric an absolute treasure.

LEFT The roll-down scrim on its steel skeleton is an enormous parasol for the yard. The house appears expanded by the fabric structure, although it serves only to keep out the rays. To be able to change the physical shape of one's environment, particularly in an urban context, is very rare indeed.

TOP Here the scrim is rolled away. The house, on a narrow corner lot, maximizes volume, light, and privacy. It is sheathed in patinated steel panels— while not a wholly American characteristic to enjoy the weathering of materials over time, this crops up more and more in new architecture.

ABOVE So as not to impinge on neighboring bungalows, the two-story house is set back from the street. It successfully appears a mix of industrial and raw—and moreover has great strength and beauty.

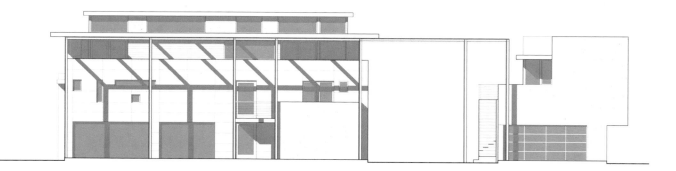

DRAWING The profile shows a strict uniformity of design—not too difficult to pass at planning level. The reality has many different layers and the result is in every sense a home. I see this house as a colorful and textured collage.

BELOW Rustproof waxed steel was used on some interior walls and ceilings. The expanse of the ground level is unified by the dark, polished concrete floor. Stern tones and varied hard textures give this house a sophisticated and urban quality.

RIGHT A glass-and-steel tension bridge spans the living area; below it are exquisite walnut open stairs inspired by Japanese *tansu* chests. Ehrlich enjoys "counterpointing a kind of primal, elemental feeling against a light, futuristic, technical experience."

Japan, where fabric and softer materials have been used for house building and shielding for thousands of years, than in the United States.

Sustainability was a major concern for the architect/owner, so concrete floors were used to absorb the sun's warmth, and windows and sliding doors designed to facilitate natural ventilation. Other materials are consciously low-maintenance recycled substances, including Trex, a compound of recycled plastic bags and sawdust usually used for decking.

The two-story residence has two parts, the smaller containing a studio and guest rooms. The building was created around the site's three mature trees and designed in layers so as not to impinge upon the street (it is scaled back from it) as other buildings are low-rise. Living and dining areas flow seamlessly together as well as outward—to the pine-shaded garden on one side and the courtyard and lap pool on the other open sides (the fourth side is a long wall clad in concrete masonry).

Ehrlich's work differs from that of other local architects in that he does not use only Western sensibility. After graduating from Rensselaer Polytechnic Institute, he joined the Peace Corps for two years and in 1969 was the first architect sent by the Corps to Morocco. For four years he traveled and studied indigenous vernacular architecture in North and West Africa, which continues to influence his approach today.

Returning to the USA in 1977, he settled in Los Angeles because it resonated for him and allowed continuing exploration into the interior/exterior connection. Seeing architecture as "a kinetic experience involving movement through space... the art of the gathering of people in humane spaces," he terms himself an "architectural anthropologist," understanding connections between "architecture and culture, people and place." Ehrlich loves to hear people wandering past his home: "In Africa you could go out and hear drumming circles," he says.

Branching out

Heir to a more casual Australian vernacular, architect John Wardle's home in the Melbourne suburb of Kew weaves together a strictly architectural structure and a cozy liveableness. Twisting and turning on its axis around the roots and trunks of three huge elm trees, it presents a sheer glass front that is almost treehouse yet undeniably urban.

Well before Frank Lloyd Wright and Ludwig Mies van der Rohe, Australians interpreted the house on a horizontal plane: not a secure and intimate enclosure from city dangers, but a simple platform-and-roof-configured shelter open to a vast expanse of nature. The idea of the veranda and living without walls defines a lineage of dwellings which is said to have begun with stick-framed, bark-topped shelters set up by wandering Aborigines, remnants of which can still be seen in the panoramic windows of many Sydney and Melbourne apartment towers. There were colonial examples, too, in Australia, in the Mediterranean-style verandas added to Georgian cottages and villas as protection from the sun. These 19th-century attachments spread rapidly from port towns to the hinterlands and outback, where they came to characterize the classic farmhouse: a square cabin surrounded by shady timber decks on which the household mostly lived and slept (this outdoorsy model remains a common inspiration in the warmer parts of Australia today).

In nature, Australia's architecture remains predominantly sparse, open shelters immaculately crafted. Whether metal or timber, "primitive huts" (if I do not manage to offend anyone by the term) built today by many of the most famous antipodean architects often appear light of foot, athletic, and

with thin skins stretched tautly over skeletal frames—at least to the outside world. (You see, we are envious in Europe of anyone with room to build, and study their efforts hard.) There are pockets of disciples of this "bush vernacular" school who consider shade and ventilation to be the crucial requirements of comfortable dwelling in the subtropics, and the architecture of many Australian houses reflects such primal necessities by either providing an expansive and extravagant-gesturing roof, a sombrero sheltering the building from sun and downpours, or by the installation of louvers (either fixed timber battens or direction-adjustable metal blades) set inside or externally, as walls or canopies, or by way of the simpler sun screen. Sun-and-breeze strategies are of less concern to architects from

BELOW LEFT Wardle's home confronts the visitor with a glass wall in a steel portal, twisted on the building's axis. The concrete shell provided an integral structural base for the new portal and the timber structure above.

BELOW Less deconstructed, more reconstructed with alignment, this house has complicated and intelligent angles that create a unique interior space. Here a lectern is formed where the floor reaches the window wall.

RIGHT The elms seem very close. For maximum protection of their root zones, like the system of building a swimming-pool shell, the site was excavated in the winter months then a concrete shell was built between two of the trees.

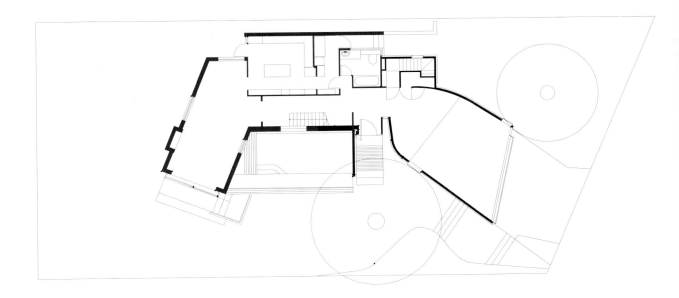

LEFT The interior is serene in white, all accent on the outside. The exterior is black oiled *Eucalyptus obliqua* (messmate), set in a board-and-batten arrangement on a doubly thick stud frame.

PLAN The house has been shaped by the trees. Explains Wardle, "The linear arrangement of the plan shifts to find a course through the spaces between the root zones."

more temperate latitudes, who need to consider gloom as much as sun: houses near Australia's south coast tend to be monumental in demeanor, with flat walls that face prevailing winds, and on opposing faces wrap around to shelter glass living areas, sundecks, and swimming pools (like Clinton Murray's Tasman House in Merimbula, see pages 74–9).

House style in Australia certainly shows variety, from coast to coast and designer to designer. John Wardle, architect of his namesake firm, exhibits much flitting from vernacular to vernacular within his own repertoire. A house for a client in Balnarring is a timber beach house, as is his Surf Coast House, yet his own home (as well as the newly built City Hill House) in the Melbourne suburb of Kew confronts us with a great glass wall as the façade of an otherwise wood-and-concrete structure. Wardle explains the discrepancy of style and how it has developed to a point: "Victoria's coastal regions are losing the architectural type of the holiday shack. Development over the past decades, fueled by increasing demand and rebuilding after the

Ash Wednesday fires, has seen the rude shacks replaced by a suburban architectural language that more closely mirrors affluence and the demands for comfort and amenity." Founded in 1986 by Wardle, the design-intensive practice has 25 staff. The firm fosters a collaborative studio environment and, unusually for the region, it works across three states, on everything from single housing and apartment buildings to universities and commercial tower blocks. Wardle has won many awards including the prestigious Sir Zelman Cowen Awards for Public Buildings.

For his own family home in the Melbourne suburbs, it seems the affluence is definitely on display for John and his wife Susan, in the nicest possible way (the success of his firm is encouraging for budding architects). Whereas in London we might keep the façade and knock down the rest (Heritage and Planning rules), the opposite seems to be the rage in the Melbourne suburbs, where this stunning glass façade is (meticulously) slapped on the front of a more demure dwelling. Extending forward from its original siting between three massive elm trees, which provide a canopy, on an elevated site above the Yarra Valley, the new spaces have been elevated as interlocking platforms that have been set over original floor levels. This device offers greater views across the city as well as affording a partially subterranean story suitable for a basement and a garage.

It is extraordinary how much attention to detail has been given to the positioning of the house vis-à-vis the trees. Wardle explains that the arrangement of the house, new spaces and extended original spaces has been affected by the position of each tree: "The linear arrangement of the plan shifts to find a course through the spaces between the root zones. The enveloping walls are, at the outer face, misaligned but both curve slightly to meet within the orthogonal framework of the original residence."

The siding system devised for the outside of the house (see caption at top of page) suggests the rhythm of the new stud framing and furthermore adds texture and rich color to the house surface, tying it to the surrounding foliage. A dramatic glass curtain wall presents to the street side, offset and twisted at its main edge so it provides a shift in vista toward city views, thus skewing the alignment of the plan's axis.

The tree canopy over the entire elevation frames the house, visually serving to separate it from its suburban setting, a sombrero of sorts but far removed from "bush vernacular." This house is a major player on the international field and one I take my hat off to!

FAR LEFT Note the curve in the wall: as seen on the plan, this is where the house shifts its axis and accommodates itself to the parameters set by the elm trees.

CENTER Despite the strict architectural lines, this is an abode for living in. Cozy spaces are evident although the interior is designed to expose the workings of the house.

LEFT Hans Wegner chairs surround a table that doubles as a home office desk, with distractingly pleasant views even at ground-floor level.

materials

In industry terms, a building envelope or "skin" consists of the structural materials and finishes used to enclose space, separating inside from outside; it includes walls, windows, doors, roofs, and floor surfaces. The envelope, any good architect or engineer will explain, must balance the house's requirements for ventilation and daylight with thermal and moisture protection appropriate to the climatic conditions of the site. It must be durable in those conditions and, as far as possible, environmentally friendly. Envelope design is a major factor in determining the amount of energy a building uses in operation, and in addition, the environmental impact and energy costs associated with production and transportation of different envelope materials vary greatly.

The most important factor affecting envelope design is climate. Dry and humid climates require very different design strategies. In a hot, dry climate, temperature fluctuations between day and night are significant, and materials with high thermal mass should be used for maximum insulation. A building material with high thermal mass and adequate wall thickness will lessen and delay the impact of temperature variations from outside on the interior. The material's high thermal capacity means it prevents heat from penetrating quickly through walls or roofs to overheat the interior, absorbing it to let out slowly when the air is cooler. Because temperature in hot, dry climates tends to fall considerably after sunset, the result is a thermal flywheel effect: the building interior is cooler than the exterior during the day and warmer than it at night. Buildings subject to diurnal fluctuations have traditionally been built with thick walls from materials with high mass such as adobe or masonry. Furthermore, windows are generally limited on most faces, with larger openings carefully positioned to avoid full-strength summer sun (which may anyway be too high in the sky to shine in), but perhaps admit some sunshine in winter when its warmth is more welcome.

 In a hot, humid climate, however, building is quite different, since night temperatures do not drop considerably below daytime highs: with no need for insulation, lighter materials with little thermal capacity, but perhaps more scope for ventilation or resistance to rot, are preferred. In some hot, moist climates, nonetheless, materials such as masonry are common, as they function as a desiccant. Roofs and walls may be protected from the sun's heat by overhangs or plant materials, which grow readily in the humidity. Here large wall openings should be positioned primarily on opposing sides of the envelope to catch breezes and encourage through ventilation.

wood

In North America, wood has long been a building material for homes of various kinds. Its wide availability and accessibility meant that the earliest European settlers used timber from the forests of New England to make their shelters. They adapted methods used by local tribes of Native Americans, and eventually evolved the basic log cabin, which in turn developed into traditional clapboard homes and sophisticated houses at least partly made of wood. Today wood is perfectly acceptable as a contemporary building material, one that is beautiful and good for us in several ways.

Many of the world's great buildings are made from wood, yet wood is often undervalued or ignored in the history of architecture. It is a material with unique qualities of form, color and structure. From the sweeping eaves of Todaiji temple in Japan (the world's largest wooden building, dating from 1709), or the Baroque blockwork of Kizhi Island's cathedral in Russia (1714) with its powerful onion domes, to the willowy iroko-wood construction by Renzo Piano for the Cultural Centre in Noumea, New Caledonia, of 1998 (which has to be one of the most modern structures on the planet), wood has shown versatility and ability to evolve in all ways, including stylistically. I was delighted to see glass-and-steel devotee Sir Norman Foster design a superlative structure of wood in Switzerland's Engadine valley a couple of years ago; sourcing material locally minimized transportation costs as well as fuel consumption. Foster is proud of these environmental credentials and I think other architects should follow suit.

Those building with wood are using the world's most renewable and environmentally friendly building product. In its 1976 report, CORRIM, the Consortium for Research on Renewable Industrial Materials, endorsed wood's energy-efficiency. In recent years, environmental concerns have joined with energy-efficiency questions, and in 1998 CORRIM examined construction and performance of houses in the cold of Minneapolis and the humid heat of Atlanta, and found use of wood in both locations presented

LEFT Solid wood flooring, and furniture offer potential generations of hard use. Their beauty is not skin-deep. They can live with nicks and scratches and are easily repaired and refinished. Coatings and finishes add to durability.

THIS PAGE This house on the Tasman Sea was painstakingly built with a team of three carpenters. Wood is a natural material that changes appearance with time and seeks balance with its surroundings.

BELOW Wood, particularly the blond or bleached variety, has become a very modern look for use in the domestic environment although timber is a material that has not always seemed at the forefront of technology in recent times.

RIGHT Plywood is used liberally in this house in France, resulting in a simple vocabulary and homogenous build. It takes confidence to apply ply to interiors since its appearance is not always the obvious or classic choice. Here it is splendid in its vastness.

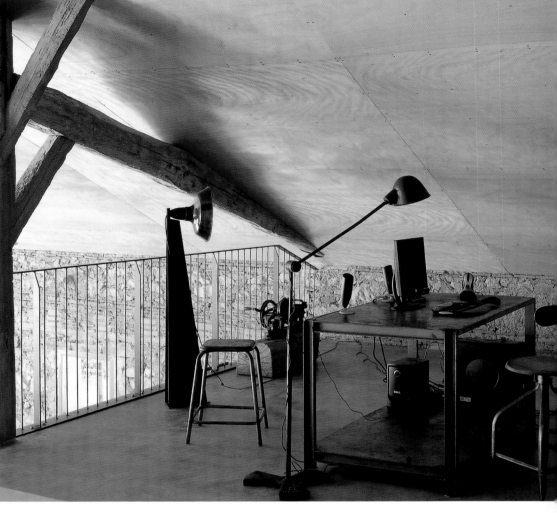

LEFT In a new build in France, beams and other structural elements are reclaimed wood, as are stair risers. The Mobile Light, which moves gently in air currents and further serves to accent the wood feature by night, is by Paul Verburg.

ABOVE A major feature of the living area in this California home has been formed by the addition of beautiful walnut *tansu*-style stairs. *Tansu* are traditional Japanese cabinets or chests, hence the stairs here also serve as storage.

ABOVE With flooring, moisture passes mainly through the end grain, so cut or mitered ends should be sealed with a transparent sealer before installation. Expansion and contraction of wood is normal during changes in the weather.

ABOVE RIGHT In a new but traditional extension to a waterside home at Goose Creek on Long Island, a very American nautical feel has been created by using painted wooden boards for walls throughout. Even these will change as they age.

significantly less environmental risks than steel- or concrete-frame options. The results demonstrated wood's benefits in almost all of five categories: embodied energy, global-warming potential, air-emission index, water emissions, and solid waste. Further research found using steel frames alone to generate 33 percent more greenhouse-gas emission than wooden ones, and concrete a staggering 80 percent more. Using wood products reduces the need to burn fossil fuels to make or transport concrete or steel. Forests can be regenerated and, while much of the carbon from a harvested forest remains in wood products, new trees remove more carbon from the air.

Aside from general environmental benefits, wood is unsuited to desert regions, where trees are scarce and wood shrinks as it dries out. In humid climates, however, although the wrong wood will rot easily, local wood can be ideal. But use of tropical hardwoods requires caution, since their felling may deplete rainforest resources that take centuries to recover.

In any hot zone, particularly a humid one, wood is at risk from insects such as termites. Prevention is better than cure—usually toxic chemicals. Treating or sealing gives some protection, but best is to avoid direct contact with the ground, through concrete, steel, or masonry foundations.

THIS PAGE Architects increasingly reveal wood in all its beauty. Exposed ceiling joists and carpentry throughout a house in New Zealand (top center) place visual emphasis on the spaces as opposed to ornament. Some alternatives to solid wood (top right) are wood veneers—thin slices of wood bonded to composite boards or plywood. This type of construction is often described as "all wood." What looks like solid hardwood may be something else: it pays to ask questions and take a hard look at materials.

ABOVE Hardwoods are deciduous trees with broad leaves, generally dormant in winter. Temperate varieties include oak, ash, cherry, maple, and poplar, while mahogany, rosewood, teak, and wenge are among the invaluable hardwoods from tropical forests. Aside from aesthetic considerations, substitutes can't compare with hardwoods when it comes to holding nails and screws and withstanding stresses and abrasions of daily life. Hardwoods for use in the home are carefully kiln-dried for that purpose, and will take on or give off moisture with extreme changes in humidity. When the air is exceptionally warm and humid, solid hardwoods absorb moisture and expand. With cooler, drier air, they give off moisture and contract. Softwoods or conifers have needles and are quick to regrow. Widely available species include cedar, fir, hemlock, pine, redwood, spruce, and cypress. In a home, softwoods are used mainly as structural lumber such as 2x4s and 2x6s, with some limited decorative applications.

stone

IN A HOT, DRY CLIMATE, NOTHING CAN BEAT THE COOL, INSULATING SOLIDITY AND DURABILITY OF A THICK STONE WALL, THE LOCAL ROCK BLENDING WITH ITS NATURAL SURROUNDINGS.

Natural stone offers weight, opacity, and a variety of patination. Not only does it look at home in its local environment, but it is suited to the climatic conditions, and hence extremely durable; and in hot, dry surroundings demanding materials with high thermal mass for insulation, it fits the bill beautifully. For these reasons, and to avoid transport costs, stone should be quarried as close to a site as possible – although small amounts of decorative rock may be transported from elsewhere.

Building with stone can nonetheless be costly and time-consuming. Just as organizing and erecting a stone castle in past centuries was a daunting task involving enormous outlays of material, manpower, time, and money, so today. But, like their forebears, new stone houses will live on and display status and substance. While stone somehow contradicted the popular image of early modernism, now contemporary architects are looking to its ancient values to give new expression to their ideas.

ABOVE View House in Knysna, South Africa, is a bastion-type sandstone structure. The sandstone within the main courtyard here has been cut into regular forms and the wall executed more like brickwork. The effect is still rough-hewn.

ABOVE RIGHT A cast-concrete bathtub from Get Real Surfaces and Charlemagne mosaic floor from Waterworks give texture to an Arizona bathroom. Limestone walls, cool to touch, accentuate other finishes and textures.

Stonemasonry originated with dry-stacked stonework, where walls are carefully layered up without mortar, gravity serving as the binder that holds everything together. Freestanding dry-stacked stone walls are usually larger at the base and taper in slowly as the height increases. For absolutely no expense but labor costs, Irish farmers would build miles upon miles of stone walls this way, and low dry-stacked stone walls are ideal for landscaping projects.

Where "mortar" was first used, it was often merely mud or limestone plaster with little strength, which functioned as calking to stop the flow of air rather than cementing stones together. Traditional mortared stone walls evolved with the emergence of cement mortar, made of burnt gypsum or lime mixed with water to make a paste with slight bonding capability. Stone walls still had to be built carefully: the paste just filled the gaps between stones and cured to form a soft, rocklike substance.

THIS PAGE Floating House in Kyalami, South Africa, by Slee & Co is a house for entertaining, almost an elliptical barge with all spaces flowing into one another and opening up directly to the water's edge. To the north is a moat-like swimming pool; here, to the south, the kitchen floats on a *koi* carp pond with a curved local-stone wall as backdrop.

The formula for modern cement originated in England in 1824. Called "Portland cement" because its color is similar to rock from the Portland peninsula, it is made with limestone or chalk calcium, plus alumina and silica from clay and shale. The ingredients are ground, burned in a kiln at about 2,500°F (1,350°C), fused into chunks, cooled, and powdered. Gypsum is added to control setting speed, sand and water mixed in for a smooth mortar, often with lime for flexibility. With Portland cement it is possible to build a tall stone wall that does not taper inward. But although stones are "glued" together, stoneworking techniques are still important. Building a stone wall is an art, requiring time and skill.

Veneered stone walls are easier to build, and most stonework today (exceptions include the houses in this book by Johann Slee and Andrzej Zarzycki) consists of a non-structural veneer of stone against a structural wall of concrete (see pages 138–41) or cinder block. The structural wall is erected first, then

ABOVE LEFT Slate covers floors inside and out (on decks) at this Napa, California, house. Hardwearing floor materials include sandstone, York stone, granite, and limestone. Slate, a dense non-porous stone that varies in color, is extremely popular but usually off-limits because of its relative cost.

ABOVE CENTER In keeping with local municipal requirements, a new build in Provence uses blocks of local limestone to create the appearance of an age-old structure.

ABOVE Entry to the Knysna courtyard, South Africa. Sandstone is a sedimentary rock composed of small grains cemented together by siliceous, felspathic, or calcareous material. Its color varies, depending on the binding material, from red through brown,

greenish, yellow, gray, and white. Durability also depends on the cementing material, while porosity varies from low to very low.

LEFT Robert Dallas's wide, low South of France houses use traditional local stone and components with total authenticity, maintaining continuity with old Provençal style while adapting to modern ways of life.

RIGHT Limestone is sedimentary rock formed at the bottom of lakes and seas with the accumulation of calcium-rich shells and bones. Calcareous stones readily dissolve in acid, so acidic products should never be used on them. Limestone that will take a polish is considered marble by most people, but if shells are visible or it is not crystalline, it is technically limestone.

LEFT In a former Italian monastery, now a home, marble dust was added to resin for the flooring, providing substance and deep texture. Pure resin, while easy to clean, might appear too plastic. The quartz aggregate means varying texture and skid-resistance.

BELOW LEFT Stone is the preferred hard surface for bathrooms, hard-wearing and easy to clean (whereas porcelain chips). It can be cut with a geometric hard edge or left *au naturel*—here a combination. Marble, limestone, and travertine are popular but costly.

BELOW CENTER Mosaics occur worldwide, often in local patterns. Here in Marrakech an outdoor water feature has a black stone mosaic backsplash. Mosaic can be hand cut and applied piece by piece, or supplied in pre-planned patterns with numbered elements.

BELOW RIGHT A hard-wearing and economic product is mosaic sold in ready-made patterns mounted on paper to make it easy to lay, or terrazzo marble chips, plain or multicolored, set in cement, and then ground to a smooth finish or left rocky.

BOTTOM The shower in the main bathroom of Johann Slee's Johannesburg house. Although much of the house is open to the elements, this is an indoor shower made to look alfresco by its dry-packed sandstone wall: a very interesting feature.

thin, flat stones are glued to its face with cement mortar. Metal tabs in the wall are mortared between stones to tie it all together and keep the stonework from peeling off. The structural wall serves as a form to make it really simple to lay the stones, provided they have good flat edges to work with.

A slipformed wall might be described as a cross between a traditional mortared stone wall and a veneered one. It is the method of stonemasonry many building firms use the most. Short forms, up to 2ft (0.6m) feet tall, are placed on both sides of a wall as a guide for stonework. Stones are then placed inside the forms, with their good profiles against the form. Then concrete is poured in behind the rocks, and reinforcing steel bars may be added for strength. This kind of wall can be faced with stone on one or both sides. With slipforms it is easy even for a novice to build a freestanding stone wall.

On one hand, stone retains a power to speak of ancient tradition; on the other, it is emblematic of the precise techniques utilized in modern structures. Many contemporary architects have explored stone architecture for civic buildings. For instance, Rafael Moneo's city hall in Murcia, Spain, was completed in 1999, while Richard Meier's Getty Center, Los Angeles, reinterprets stone as siding, and Ortner and Ortner's Museum for Modern Art in Vienna (2001) uses stone differently again, as an extreme interpretation of the most contemporary museum—the rectilinear form and color of the anthracite standing out against Vienna's less radical museum quarter.

The 20th century saw a shift in relationship between architecture and stonemasonry, as architects became disengaged from the ancient craft of creating. Our culture must now redress this: architects should be willing to work alongside stone specialists and explore once more the nature of "stacking," which is an intrinsic part of building with stone since it involves the spaces between the stone. Then we may begin to see more buildings where "stoniness" is a feature, not merely a building material.

earth & brick FAR MORE PREVALENT THAN STONE WALLS IN PARTS OF THE WORLD SUCH AS AFRICA, CHINA, SOUTHEAST ASIA, AND MUCH OF INDIA IS MUD, IN ALL ITS TACTILE, COOLING GLORY.

The insulation qualities of mud are supreme—it is packed with air—and it is just lovely to the touch of the hand. Transportation costs are almost nil, and while generally not as durable as stone, earthen structures do last. The American government recently documented over 350,000 currently extant earthen houses and structures in the USA: many have survived with minimal maintenance for the past hundred years, and some were built as long ago as the 1600s.

Earthen buildings encompass a wide range, from those of simple rammed earth (which has low tensile strength and must usually be reinforced), through earth plaster over other cores, to the use of earthen bricks of many kinds (baked by the sun or in a kiln), including rustic adobe and clay-based brick. Soils themselves come in many guises, as any potter or gardener will tell you, some much more alkaline than others. It is this variability that makes multistoryed earthen buildings possible in the High Atlas of North

Africa or in northern Yemen, for example, but not in other regions. Soils formed under coniferous forests are extremely acidic and unsuitable for building, whereas those in deciduous forest or grassland can be widely used for construction, as in Western Europe and North America.

Desert soils, with their relatively high sand content, make an effective building material, while the arid heat greatly assists drying of bricks. Such earth bricks are common in the Middle East, North Africa, parts of Europe (notably Spain), and parts of the Americas. The Arabs brought their technique of *atobe*—making sun-dried bricks—to Spain, where it became adobe, as it is known through Hispanic America and increasingly worldwide. Adobe is essentially building with mud and straw, and can go horribly wrong unless the rules, derived from centuries of experience, are adhered to.

Blocks of adobe may be hand-molded, but using molds produces sharper edges and standard dimensions, facilitating bonding. Bricks are molded in a

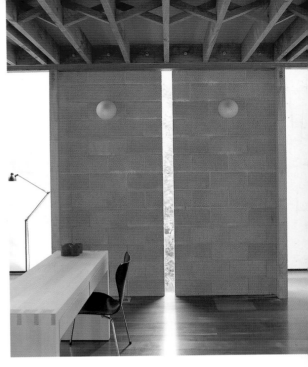

OPPOSITE All openings in rammed-earth walls must have lintels to span the opening and support the earth above. Thick walls may need special detailing to accommodate manufactured windows.

ABOVE FAR LEFT Brick, made from clay and sand, is highly recyclable. Reclaimed brick, available through salvage companies, is often desired for its weathered appearance. Damaged brick can be crushed and recycled, to make more brick or for landscaping.

ABOVE LEFT & ABOVE Walls of hollow concrete blocks in bricklike

configuration work well in areas of seismic activity like New Zealand (above) and California (above left). Steel rods are inserted into the hollow blocks and wet concrete poured around them. Once hardened, it has great strength.

FAR LEFT & LEFT Waterproof finishes for soil-based materials such as cement stucco are more permanent but expensive, and trap moisture, which may be problematic. Permeable finishes such as mud plaster are less durable but inexpensive, and allow walls to absorb and give off airborne moisture.

simple wooded frame, usually thin and square, then knocked out and stacked on end to dry. In building, the bricks are bonded by a wet mud of the same consistency, so bricks and mud dry and weather at the same rate. These bricks behave much like stone when they dry out, and if not well compacted they shear and crack easily. Consequently, adobe is mainly used for load-bearing walls in compression, but it is not unusual to see it employed in other ways—including timberless domes that utilize the corbeling technique (in Syria, for example), where the building forms are egglike in section, efficiently distributing the stresses.

Adobe is often finished with a plaster of mud and straw to give a smooth, rendered surface, reducing wind erosion. Some countries, such as Iran, favor dung as an emulsifying covering: this combination mud plaster is called *kargel*. With time, each region has developed its own method of constructing with mud. To bind well for building, soils must contain larger pieces of coarse sand as well as small sand particles, silt, and fine clay. Clay is mixed with water and straw or similar material and mashed to the right consistency. Hybrid adobe is a revolutionary building material used to

create low-cost insulated homes and other structures. It combines recycled paper with earth, sand, and a binder to create a sustainable, inexpensive, strong, fibered material that can be poured, sprayed, or sculpted.

While on the subject of earth, I think it important to mention "earth coupling": the percentage of a building's skin in contact with the earth. From season to season, even in a relatively constant warm climate, air temperatures can fluctuate greatly. Unlike air, earth maintains practically constant temperatures year-round, and the deeper you dig into the earth, the more constant and moderate the temperature. Thus insulation efficiency increases with the depth of the earth connection, and excavated earth is often then piled up against exterior walls to deflect winds, reduce air infiltration, and increase the depth of earth coupling.

Recently mud has become fashionable in urban settings. Architect Glenn Murcutt, for example, in Sydney began to build massive walls of rammed earth and raw concrete in the late 1980s, moving away from steel-and-glass shoeboxes. Mud is seeing a resurgence as a building material worldwide, with the masters leading the way, and it is a truly delightful one.

glass

GLASS IS CRISP AND GIVES GORGEOUS REFLECTIONS, PARTICULARLY IN CITYSCAPES. DESPITE HEATING UP, IT CAN BE USED TO REGULATE INDOOR TEMPERATURE AS WELL AS PROVIDING A WINDOW ON THE WORLD OUTSIDE.

It might seem that people who live in glass houses should not live in warm climates, since large areas of glass trap the sun's heat, making it difficult to maintain ambient temperature (and we do not want to rely on air conditioning, do we?). That steamy, greenhouselike effect is even greater in humid regions. Yet windows can mean ventilation, valuable in both dry and humid heat, and a dark, glassless building is just not appealing, not to mention wasting the sun's energy. The trick is to find a balance and to use glass cleverly as well-positioned windows for optimum views while encouraging it to work in your house's (and bank balance's) favor.

Glass has advantages in a warm climate, since it can help to reduce energy costs by drawing in the sun, carefully, to maintain a stable interior temperature. There are various ways of doing this, be it

LEFT Brick, wood, or concrete walls are characterized by surface, glass by depth. Glass walls define space but do not enclose it, going against the grain of interior versus exterior. This house is 90% glazed.

ABOVE Used cleverly, glass can even out heat. A building benefits from "direct gain" when solar rays pass through a window and warm a surface in a living space. The more exposed to the sun, the greater the gain.

TOP RIGHT In Arizona, 19ft (5.8m) of floor-to-ceiling glass reveals the wilderness. Today we can have glass that is climate sensitive, or that allows insiders to see out but is opaque to passersby—not an issue here.

ABOVE RIGHT In Steven Ehrlich's California home, a glass-and-steel tension bridge spans the living area. The house maximizes volume and light, the glass bridge adding transparency to an open-plan room.

through solar panels (which can be mightily expensive) or the "passive" methods considered here. Essentially, passively heated and cooled buildings rely on sun, wind, and surrounding earth to maintain comfortable interior temperatures. Hence orientation plays an enormous part in window design.

For the best passive solar performance, the area of sun-facing glazing should be 7 to 12 percent of a building's floor area; many successful California houses, for instance, have approximately 12 percent window area to the south (since this is the northern hemisphere) and 2–3 percent on east, west, and north sides. Overhangs can be key, providing shade for sun-facing windows in summer yet allowing low-angled sun to penetrate in winter when more heat is needed; they are not so useful for east- or west-facing windows since sun from the east or west is low in the sky (nor nearer the tropics, where summer sun is overhead). Of course we do not all seek passive solar gain: some homes have their main windows positioned precisely to avoid direct sun, while others give priority to views, but hot homes rarely invite heat in indiscriminately with large windows on all sides.

A more complex way of warming interiors is the thermal-storage wall, typically a dark masonry wall positioned between exterior glazing and living space. It absorbs the sun's rays by day and radiates heat in the evening when it is cooler. Thermal-storage walls occupy little space and are particularly effective in winter, when low sun angles strike them most directly. Another energy-saving device is "sun spaces," glass rooms built onto the sunny side of a building to collect heat, like a conservatory. These rooms are thermally isolated from the rest of the building so their interiors heat quickly. The hot air is released directly into the building via windows, doors, or vents. Such spaces can, for example, speed early-morning warm-up in a climate where nights are cool, such as a desert environment.

Solar windows increase the insulating properties of glass. These are double-glazed windows with twice the R-value (the measurement of thermal resistance) of single-glazed. A new type with a thin film between the glass layers that reflects long-wave radiation has an R-value over four times that of single glazing. If the space between the glass is filled with argon gas, the R-value can double again.

Specialty window coatings can boost the energy efficiency of windows. The "low-E2" variety is good for hot climates because, in addition to improving the insulating ability of windows, it limits solar heat gain by blocking infrared and some ultraviolet rays. In some cases, solar-control glass can reduce cooling loads so much that cooling-system capacity can be cut or glass area added without increasing the loads. It offers the greatest energy savings where cooling costs are higher than heating costs.

ABOVE Oh, the luxury of a picture window in one's bathroom. There are numerous courtyards in this Marrakech home, and much of the house is in relative shade. The window makes the most of courtyard privacy.

ABOVE This New Zealand house has a glazed screen with an expressed colonnade stretching between block walls. Wooden shields, with strips of glass louver, give shelter from summer sun (and neighbors).

RIGHT Just as a structural overhang can keep out summer sun but allow in low-angled winter rays, so in Johann Slee's South African house, trees provide natural shelter. The picture window draws the outside in.

concrete

A PLIABLE AND POETIC MATERIAL, IN MANY CASES, PARTICULARLY WHEN USED WITH OTHER MATERIALS, CONCRETE HAS A SURPRISING LIGHTNESS OF TOUCH. ALTHOUGH THERE ARE ENVIRONMENTAL ISSUES, IT HAS POTENTIAL FOR HOT-CLIMATE BUILDING.

LEFT In the underbelly of the house built by Helena Arahuete in Napa, California, concrete plays a major role—only the floor is slate. Concrete walls mimic the knotted wood that supported them in construction.

ABOVE Pigment can be added to concrete for color—it does not have to be the usual gray. Here the floor is anthracite-colored concrete.

ABOVE RIGHT Some people prefer a rough-hewn look and choose to leave a poured floor

pitted and mottled on the surface. Concrete is frequently used alongside earth in builds since its stability affords earth greater strength and the two sit well together.

ABOVE FAR RIGHT Others like to contrast different concrete finishes—polished concrete is popular as it is easy to sweep and wash. It can give a clinical edge to a room or just a more polished one in every sense. Concrete floors are extremely durable if correctly made.

Among the worries and concerns for global warming, we have a serious problem with concrete. Although it behaves beautifully in a warm climate—it is good for insulation, absorbing and storing warmth, and highly durable (plus resistant to insects), even in heat or humidity—and is relatively inexpensive and quicker to build with than stone or other laborious methods, its production certainly does not help the environment. Concrete is used pretty indiscriminately for public and private builds and contributes an estimated massive 10–12 percent of carbon dioxide emissions in the world, due to a combination of sheer volume produced and the very high temperatures required to create the core Portland cement (see page 126) used in the standard process.

Concrete consists of Portland cement mixed with sand, gravel, and water. The larger particles of gravel interlock like little fingers to make the concrete resistant to cracking. Steel reinforcing bar, can be added to serve as much longer fingers. Vast amounts of energy are required for the blast furnaces making cement, and this comes most often from burning coal. Attempts at energy-efficiency and CO_2 reduction in the cement industry have been, up to now, concentrated on small improvements in furnace technology and replacing coal with waste oil and other refuse where possible (and profitable).

Great amounts of CO_2 are also released as concrete dries. This de-gassing is a result of the key reaction in hardening, so it has been widely assumed that there is no possibility for improvements. But at Luleå University in Sweden, a Russian guest researcher has spearheaded a new grinding process for cement and sand which cracks the grains so that they add more effectively to the strength of the concrete, and the quantity of cement can be reduced by half without compromising strength. This new technology reduces emissions radically, both in production and during curing. Since it is also profitable, there is a good chance of decreasing the world's CO_2 emission by about 3 percent just by its use.

Alternatives to traditional concrete include some which take less energy to make, have better thermal properties, or make use of materials which otherwise would have become landfill. But each has its drawbacks, typically in cost—one reason why concrete remains so popular is economy. Recently, however, CSIRO, the Australian science and industrial research office, announced the development of a form of concrete called HySSIL. According to Dr Swee Liang Mak, who leads the CSIRO team, "HySSIL is a revolutionary aerated cementitious [cement-based] product that is as strong as normal concrete but is only half as heavy. It provides up to five times the thermal insulation of concrete and is also impact and fire resistant. HySSIL wall panels are also expected to offer significant cost advantages over existing products." HySSIL is easier to recycle than traditional concrete, more resistant to earthquakes (because of lower density and lighter weight), and is made of non-toxic material. The lower cost comes from a combination of lower energy use for manufacturing and lower transportation expenses because of its light weight; the latter also greatly reduces the cost of use.

In a warm climate, building with any type of concrete has pitfalls and needs tight control. Hot-weather problems include quicker drying and evaporation, so more water is used, reducing potential strength; it may mean less air within the concrete, hence less insulation; and fast setting times may be inconvenient. But on the whole concrete is durable, adaptable, and has high thermal mass—particularly advantageous in a climate that is warm by day and cooler at night.

A year or two ago I would have thought twice about advocating use of concrete (since I have three children, I am mightily concerned for the environment). But with some concretes now developed that actively absorb CO_2, I am having a change of heart. Although it will take a lot to educate the industry to be as environmentally aware as it should be, concrete need no longer be the bad apple of building.

BELOW FAR LEFT High temperature, wind, and humidity can all have a negative impact on concrete's performance, although higher humidity tends to reduce the effects of heat. Concrete is used here in a three-story essentially earth house.

BELOW LEFT Concrete may crack due to a rapid drop in temperature, for instance if a slab or wall is placed on a very hot day, followed by a cool night typical of desert. Trust the experts if you require a flawless floor.

BELOW During building, heat makes water evaporate from concrete surfaces more quickly and the concrete stiffens earlier, increasing the chances of plastic cracking. Scoring helps prevent mass cracks.

RIGHT For successful placement of concrete in hot climes, be sure you have enough workers to avoid delays placing, finishing, and curing, and consider early-morning or evening placement. That said, stairs are relatively easily constructed in concrete.

metal

WE TEND TO ASSUME THAT METAL HEATS UP TOO READILY FOR USE IN A HOT CLIMATE—THE CLASSIC HOT TIN ROOF—BUT WITH THE RIGHT FINISH IT WILL REFLECT THE SUN AND HELP PREVENT A HOUSE FROM OVERHEATING. IT IS ALSO LIGHT, CHEAP, AND DURABLE.

It was not until selecting projects for this book that I began to understand the advantages of using metal in a hot climate; I was frankly surprised to see it so readily applied, for example, as roofing in the dry Arizona heat or for window frames in dusty Marrakech. Metal has a low thermal mass, so does not store heat by day and release it at night. But with the right structure and finish (such as white paint), it will deflect the sun's rays, and can also be made to transfer heat to water supplies.

Metal's predominant—although not only—use in hot-climate builds is for roofing. Metal roofing has a very long history, with roofs in the United

OPPOSITE Whether used for window frames, roofing, or anywhere around the house, paint finishes on metal shed dirt and do not support the growth of algae or fungal matter, which is particularly important if the climate is humid. Paints used on "cool" metal roofing also resist chalking and color fade.

ABOVE LEFT, TOP In Provence, a unique and artful security door is hand-forged iron. Because of metal's malleability, it can provide a decorative option even when fulfilling a primary function. The grille-like effects formed by metal, whether forged, woven, or laser-cut, add an element of airiness to a warm house.

ABOVE LEFT, BOTTOM There are definite advantages in selecting metal over wood for door and window frames: a wooden window frame weathers with age, and expands and contracts according to weather conditions. It also requires three times more material than a metal frame, reducing the glazed area.

ABOVE The long life and low maintenance of metal roofing, combined with savings from energy efficiency, give it a very attractive life-cycle cost. Whereas unfinished (i.e., natural silver-colored) metal absorbs heat too readily, many finishes reflect and radiate it well.

States that date back to the 1800s still in service. Its durability (metal roofing products being manufactured today carry manufacturers' warranties lasting from 20 to 50 years) makes them a very low per-annum-cost option, and most new products are designed so that they can be refurbished on site for additional life. Painted metal roofs retain 95 percent of their initial reflectance and emittance over time.

Another plus is that metal (at 40–135lb per 100sq ft/18–61kg per 9.3sq m) is the lightest-weight roofing available for a serious build. This has a twofold benefit: it places less demand on a building's structure and is advantageous in locations prone to seismic activity—as indeed many hot regions are. In addition, the interlocking or active fastening of most modern metal roofing panels means that severe winds can pass through them without causing any damage.

Many metal roofs are formed in ways that stop heat transfer through conduction, by allowing only minimal contact between the metal and the underlying structure. "Cool" roofs, in various finishes, combine high solar reflectance and infrared emittance to keep the roof cool while protecting against sun damage and extending roof life.

LEFT Metal door frames require much less maintenance than wood. Metal is a durable material, and metal products are not subject to the degradation experienced by organic materials when exposed to moisture. Metal has a long life thanks to its ability to resist the elements, and a low maintenance cost.

ABOVE Aesthetically speaking, metal has extensive design flexibility and can be worked to suit many different styles of building due to its ability to accept coatings of various colors and patterns. These wooden interior doors are covered in metal sheeting for subtle decorative effect.

ABOVE RIGHT, TOP On an environmental note, of which there are many in this chapter, metals are 100% recyclable if they are ever removed. Additionally, many metals used in new builds will have recycled content varying from 25% to 95%. Metal structure is light-weight and easy to install.

ABOVE RIGHT, BOTTOM Metal's building benefits are far greater than most people think in a hot climate. Just as we now appreciate its use in kitchens, where it is wipe-clean, and bug-free if cleaned regularly, so we are coming to see that it can be invaluable elsewhere in a hot home.

color

Colors may have to work well in both the brightest of days and the

Light plays a significant part in the appearance of color. In hot climates the light is brighter, so these sunnier climes produce a very different view of color from that in duller temperate conditions. Thus the use of color is different in a hot home.

Color is the most plastic of design elements and the most mutating. In any climate, it undergoes metamerism, the phenomenon by which colors alter appearance when viewed in different light conditions. An ocher hue, for example, will seem radically redder in a room lit by warm candescent lighting than its almost yellow-green appearance in a bright office space illuminated with cool fluorescent lighting. Cooler lighting sucks the blood out of beige, taupe, grays, celadon, lilac, and otherwise pleasant neutral tones; warmer lighting invigorates them. Metamerism occurs also in daylight, as colors alter depending upon season, time of day, and direction of light.

In the bright light of hotter climes, colors may vary even more, as some are leached and others thrive. Many bold hues that would be overwhelming elsewhere meet their match where the sun beats down, and contrasting colors, or brusque white palaces sharpened with clean lines of bold primary accent color, often look fabulous and appropriate. In addition, allowance must be made for the effects of sun damage or fading: sunlight contains wavelengths of infrared light, which dehydrates and wears out sensitive materials, and ultraviolet whose effect, quite different, causes some pigments to fade, so they will not remain so bold.

 On the other hand, while some inhabitants of hot homes drench themselves in sunshine, others create protective shade, and here, especially if the sun is high in the sky and cannot seep in horizontally, color requirements are different again. Many proponents of hot, sunshine living keep their interiors under-lit, by daylight or artificial light, and choose hues for very subtle differences in mood.

 In any case, what happens when daylight fades will always be an issue. Colors may have to work well in both the brightest of days and the dimmest of nights, and not all will react the same way. The Purkinje effect (named after a scientist) explains that in dim lighting the human eye can see the violet/blue end of the spectrum better than reds, so red will be the first to turn gray, while blue takes on brightness. Thus although both bright blues and reds are widely used in hot homes, their impact differs markedly. The right color harmonies will deliver visual interest and a sense of logicality and order, stimulating our brains neither too much nor too little.

natural

THE NEUTRAL, NATURAL TONES OF LOCAL EARTH AND WOOD
WILL ALWAYS BE AT HOME IN THE LOCALITY OF THEIR BIRTH,
EXUDING A SENSE OF PEACE AND STABILITY.

ABOVE, TOP An otherwise unadorned corridor has stripes painted in earthen tones from dado level down, which adds curiosity and, like the wearing of hooped as opposed to striped fabric, gives visual girth to the passageway.

ABOVE, LEFT In these locations, we often came across kitchens in dark, murky colors that seemed odd to our northern sense of stark white cleanliness. This stunning taupe mottled effect links the kitchen to the rest of the house.

ABOVE Natural pigment means the color of soil, which of course differs depending upon location. Although a solid wall's color will remain stable, as here, prehistoric cave paintings prove that even surface pigment can be permanent.

RIGHT In this traditional Moroccan-style guesthouse in the grounds of a highly contemporary home, walls are simple, the floor is stained wood, the rug elephant hair. Velvet pillows add a breath of color to neutral hues.

A house build using earth and natural elements is often described as being "colored with pigment" or having "pigmented" walls, which is a little misleading as a description because pigment is not the exclusive term for natural minerals blended with earth to color walls. All paint contains pigment, mixed with a "vehicle" or liquid medium. Pigments can be obtained from naturally occurring earth colors or alternatively prepared by chemical manufacturing processes—white, for example, is made from basic carbonates, titanium oxide, or zinc sulfide or others. Neutral tones found in hot homes are generally created from naturally occurring pigments as opposed to the manufactured variety, and many are more than skin deep, since walls will be the same color all the way through if they have been created from soil.

Natural tones are born from landscape. Yellow ocher comes from a clay colored by iron and is used to produce a variety of earthy yellow shades. Umber contains ferric oxide, lime, aluminum, and manganese, and turns the warm red-brown of burnt umber when heated. Terracotta, which means "cooked earth," is found in shades that range right across the earthy spectrum from palest plaster-pink through dark reddish-brown, depending on the color of the local soil.

An interior of little color—or rather neutral color—can have a very relaxing effect since browns and earthy colors are grounding and supportive. (But avoid gray unless highly textured or concrete, since a large area of gray is neither hot nor cold as a color and, although a great supporting color for other

ABOVE, TOP Nature inspires a warm-climate palette and used to be the only source of color. Ocher, umber, and sienna were obtained from clay; madder and indigo from plants; cochineal from crushed beetles.

ABOVE The African palette also embraces the colors of the spice trade: bright yellow of turmeric, gold of saffron, rich browns of cinnamon and nutmeg. As spices can be unexpectedly cooling, so can pigment.

ABOVE, TOP Many fibers can be hand-woven to dramatic effect. Hemp, banana fiber, and corn fiber give quite different natural colors. In India alone, 12.5 million hand-weavers need marketing support for viability.

ABOVE A wool carpet in a South African game lodge is neutral in color, bleached and dyed to attain this "natural" oatmeal color—a splendid background enhancer to the dark wood of the furnishings.

ABOVE, TOP An attractive wall of eucalyptus or *latte* as it is known locally in South Africa. Even when wood tones are very dark, no two are the same; you can see movement, pattern, and light under the surface.

ABOVE Andrzej Zarzycki supports local crafts-people. These grass window treatments were made by local women, the leather tie and wooden toggle also by artisans. The straw is untreated.

hues, is flat and lifeless in sunlight.) On the other hand, surrounding yourself with over-murky tones can reflect and generate confusion or depression, according to color theorists and therapists. This can be relieved by inclusion of a few lighter or brighter colors; for example, the interior of Johann Slee's house in South Africa contains many bright accent drops by way of his paintings and the flowers in abundance around the house; earthy hues work well with the warmer oranges and reds, generally, and sometimes yellow. As a rule of thumb, the purer the hue, the healthier its effect. The neutral hues found here are merely the pigments of the surrounding soil, or at least a close neighbor. Using wood in its natural state is another easy, and often soothing, way to introduce a natural palette.

BELOW Terracotta lies at the heart of the earthy color palette. In a wide range of shades, it features throughout the Mediterranean and North Africa.

subtle

WITH A LITTLE SKILL, A LIGHT COLOR SCHEME
NEED NOT BE NORDIC OR WINTERY; PALE,
SUBTLE SHADES CAN BRING A NOTE OF AIRY
GRACE INTO EVEN SULTRY HEAT.

THIS PAGE Color schemes
can help merge old and
new styles. A 1960s Long
Island cottage
transformed by architect
Annabel Selldorf has
subtle accent color in a
Berber rug, original
Fornasetti chairs, and
ocher and green
furnishings.

OPPOSITE Graham Head
and his wife Barbara
Rathborne have
sympathetically restored
a wooden house at
Goose Creek, Long Island,
New York. A north-facing
bedroom is painted
cornflower blue, a
popular tranquil color for
waterside living.

Pale people are generally considered to be winter people: they wear a lot of black and avoid the sun. I suppose I am one of them (although I prefer desert to any other terrain, for its openness), since I don't sunbathe at all and use my children's factor-40 sun-protection cream. I remember a vision I witnessed on many an evening at the delightful Piscine Deligny when I lived in Paris in the 1990s (the Piscine was a 1930s swimming pool on a collection of barges that eventually sank into the Seine). Regularly at sundown, a very pale woman would strip to her bathing suit and walk the length of the pool in a large hat before plunging in. The *fashionista* Victoria Fernandez, as I now know it was, went to extremes to avoid the sun but enjoyed the summer heat.

A pale house interior has similar characteristics in that it has a certain demure quality that real sun-worshippers lack, and a little politesse. In addition, pale colors minimize visual fatigue and help to relax the body, consequently making good spa interiors.

Of course, white is in many ways the ideal for hot living, since it reflects heat and light, and makes one feel cooler. But the all-white house, interior and out, is not really a viable option in such climates: it would reflect the sun to a dazzling extent and would be dreadfully monotonous, at least without skillful accenting. So we need to consider pale as an accessible option, for example, if the house is to be rented out from time to time or shared with other family members who may not share the same taste.

The subtle interior will always be the most accessible—and fortunately, in a warm climate, subtlety in the form of some pale colors can be just the ticket. But be careful, since pale shades that are very close together can be uninteresting, so bland that the witness is not engaged in any manner, or may seem chaotic so that the brain cannot interpret what it sees.

When choosing colors, particularly cool ones, assess their hues, chroma level (or intensity, even if pale), light reflectance value (LRV), and the contrasts between them. LRV tells you the percentage of light reflected back by a color. In dark conditions, high reflectance reduces the need for artificial lighting, but in a bright climate the main concern may well be the reverse: too reflective a surface may dazzle and create glare. Lighter hues are more reflective than dark ones.

OPPOSITE Against a cool, pale backdrop, painted metal frames delineate the opening to outdoors and an arbor. Ocher is a popular choice for those intermediate moments—the pause between outside and in. Wooden chairs add a hint of warmth.

ABOVE LEFT The Goose Creek house has views over a sprawling lawn and the creek. The pale but definite colors are classic country and add serenity to the home.

FAR LEFT This upper-level studio is painted refreshing builders' white and anchored by a Jacques Adnet daybed

and Serge Mouille light. Subtlety comes with the hint of red accent color by way of the chair, without which it might appear clinical. The house is packed with serious collectibles.

ABOVE A home devoid of interior color, giving precedence to form, is a must for many architects; this house, in Merimbula, Australia, is by Clinton Murray.

LEFT The dining room in the Goose Creek home. The carefully chosen pale color scheme adds gentle support. Stark white interiors can sometimes be too cutting-edge for family life.

bold

STRONG COLORS SPRING TO LIFE IN
BRIGHT LIGHT, AND A SUCCESSFUL BOLD
COLOR SCHEME CAN HAVE A POTENTLY
UPLIFTING IMPACT ON HUMAN
EMOTIONS.

A bold scheme often starts with white, which is not a color as such but an absence of color, and then bold strokes are used in contrast. Such accent color is a good choice for a hot-climate home, since it combines the benefits of largely white schemes with a splash of vivacity. Color can help move the eye in a different direction, too, so, like light, it aids in the navigation of a house. Bold splashes of color also promote speed and efficiency, according to the experts—orange in a dining room is believed to encourage eating, for example.

Some hues that would be just too much in temperate lands will thrive in the sun, while others may become overpowering. Red is always powerful (and in some cultures lucky), perhaps for its association with blood as much as its strong visual impact. Bright blues are widely favored in hot lands: although some fade easily, many cope well with the variety of light conditions (the Virgin Mary is often dressed

ABOVE To break up a white space, doors can be painted. Bold strokes can be made by color-coding according to room function – teal-blue doors for bathrooms, for example, and reddish-browns for relaxation spaces.

ABOVE RIGHT US landscape architect Steve Martino has a reputation for pioneering work with native plants. A recurring theme is juxtaposition of manmade elements and ecological process; blue pigment features heavily.

RIGHT Blue makes a popular bold statement alongside white. Here in Ibiza, cobalt white contrasts with indigo walls. Indigo pigment can fade rapidly in sunlight unless worked in tempera or beneath varnish.

THIS PAGE The angle of this wall is enhanced by its bold oxblood color, lit by sunlight from a skylight. Other walls in the house are cementious and sand-colored. This wall is simply a statement, an overture to a dramatic house.

in blue, for example, in dimly lit chapels because blue retains much of its intensity even in penumbra, so she shines above all else). In times past, ultramarine pigment used to be rare, as it was produced by grinding down semiprecious lapis lazuli; today one source for indigo blue is woad, although perhaps surprisingly the E-coli bacterium can also produce it.

Color is the first thing you notice about a room, so if you are eager to go bold, make sure you are really convinced before committing yourself to a decorative scheme. No one says, "Did you see that room with the picture window and metal beams?" No, they say, "Did you see the green room?" So please make sure it is a green room you wish to be remembered for; in my opinion the most successful hot houses beg the phrase, "Did you see the view?"—the mark of a true genius build.

LEFT In Karim El Achak's Moroccan guesthouse, red plays a starring role. Iron-oxide pigments have constituted the basic palette of artisans from Egypt to India and China since history began, with associations of blood or good luck.

BELOW FAR LEFT Flat painted gray is often unwelcoming, but charcoal mottled-textured walls can be quite special—like the best flannel suit. Used dramatically in its darkest guise, gray is a good mental shelter.

BELOW LEFT Just as cool colors encourage rest and meditation, hot colors promote activity. However, too much of the red spectrum can be distracting and draining, so use it carefully, particularly in hot climes.

BELOW Muriel Brandolini's Hampton Bays home is awash with color: no surprise, since the French-Vietnamese-Venezuelan designer is renowned for her color sense. She admits to using an "ocean of bright paint" throughout her waterfront house.

furnishing

Some of the most diverse and dynamic regions of the world boast hot homes set in bucolic landscapes. Distinct architectural traditions have evolved from geographical, cultural, and historical circumstances, including imports—architectural and furnishings—from Holland, Spain, and England, of sometimes dubious appropriateness to their new climate (some elements just do not travel well). It is best, in many cases, to leave them at home and start afresh with new eyes. Contemporary modern houses in these disparate lands have common threads in that they tend to share an openness and sympathetic spirit with the tenets of modernism while remaining true to the particulars of place. The modernist house is fluid, informal, spacious, with porous boundaries between indoor and out; it is a good blueprint for interior form to follow.

Italian architect and furniture designer Antonio Citterio has much to say about building in the more remote parts of the world. Australians, he says, "focus on the real qualities and values in their life—family, relationships, food, the natural. I like these people who do not seem under stress," he adds, "unlike, for example, New Yorkers."

It is an easy-going attitude that shapes the way we live in a hotter climate, a more relaxed arena in general. We build homes for socializing, so we need a good sofa or two, a decent table to eat at, even if it is outside, good bathrooms, and perhaps an outdoor shower for that feeling of freedom, of being at one with nature. The great outdoors is usually the starting point for a hot home, and the design upshot is a deep-seated sensitivity to landscape. Use devices that bring outdoors in; blur the boundary. Indigenous materials, we know, work well in tropical and subtropical climates, as they do everywhere, but further concern must be given to the rareness of some materials, including hardwoods. The increasing use of bamboo, for example, in interior design, is encouraging and hopeful: with its rapid growth and excellent durability, it is the logical replacement for many rare woods, and with the development of techniques that allow the manufacture of flat sheets of material from bamboo canes, the idea of bamboo design has taken on a more solid shape.

As with the shells of buildings, technology coupled with sensitivity to natural materials, including fabrics, should be the guiding force for interiors. Currently it is primarily people with artistic drive and ideas of their own who design furniture using materials such as bamboo. Soon, I am sure, *haute couture* and mass-market designers will catch up, and we will see even slicker interiors made from appropriate materials.

cooking & eating

FOOD AND SHELTER ARE
OUR MOST FUNDAMENTAL
NEEDS, AND THE HISTORY
OF FOOD CAN TELL THE
STORY OF TIME AND PLACE.

The communal nature of eating, once a norm for us all, seems to have endured better for some reason in warmer climates than in temperate lands. Perhaps it is that the heat makes us prone to pause a while in the shade and ingest slowly, rather than refueling on the run while multi-tasking. Eating outdoors certainly adds to the pleasure.

It is quite incredible how centuries ago people wandered the planet sharing ideas, and changed foreign palettes by introducing spices, exotic fruits, and customs—and how just the breaking of bread together can initiate peace. Istanbul was once the beating heart of the Ottoman Empire, a crossroads where civilizations and cultures from Europe, Asia, and the Middle East met and traded. Discovering culinary delights played a significant role wherever the Ottomans traveled. They would carry with them their *kazan*, a large cooking pot in which all the ingredients collected on their journeys were

ABOVE A central work-station results in an airy kitchen with sightlines. Better to face guests or empty space than a wall. Good design is essential to a kitchen; the triangle philosophy (sink, fridge, stove), from 1950s studies in ergonomics, works well.

RIGHT In Marrakech the KO team created a cave-like kitchen that is very functional, a blend of old

techniques and modern form. A modern *tadelak* equivalent, varnished concrete, gives a brutal but shimmering effect. Cabinet doors are uncut sardine-can sheets.

OPPOSITE Marble and stainless steel evoke cleanliness and cool. Again in Morocco, we find double square basins and workstation, and space for two or three people to work at once.

A little spit and polish was all it took to clean up this kitchen in the original part of a converted 1960s American house. Keeping a kitchen neat must be effortless, and utensils should be kept to the bare minimum.

cooked over an open fire. The *kazan* offered a rich tapestry of tastes and pleasures, many influences and kitchen tips coming into play. The fusion of history and taste is an extremely palatable one.

Certain foods have had an amazing influence on history. Potatoes, for instance, indigenous to South America, were probably brought to Europe around 1570, but were widely resisted. Until 1780, they were excluded from prudent French tables, as they were thought to cause leprosy. Devout Scottish Presbyterians refused to eat them because they weren't mentioned in the Bible, while in colonial Massachusetts they were considered the spoor of witches. Ireland was the first country to fully adopt the potato, and suffered terribly in the potato famine of 1845, triggering a wave of emigration.

Despite all the to-ings and fro-ings of food throughout history, my mother tells me she saw her first banana in England only as a late teenager around 1950, and I remember clearly my own experience in Paris, aged 11, when I discovered, to my great chagrin, that Diet Coke had not yet reached French soil! Food habits generally move quite swiftly, however, and I am glad to say that the house owners who kindly allowed us to photograph their homes for this book all seem to experiment with local flavors and buy local produce, thus doing their bit for the environment by reducing transportation. Moreover, they all understood that in a warm climate, cleanliness is particularly close to godliness.

One of the most interesting aspects of photographing this book was the lunch break: although we rarely expected it, we were given lunch while working (this might have had something to do with the

OPPOSITE, BELOW In a new build in Provence, the entire kitchen is custom-designed and handmade: it leads from dining room to hallway and reception, in true French *enfilade* spirit, thus it has to be smart. Even the trash can is wood-encased, Shaker-like, designed by Andrzej Zarzycki.

RIGHT Architect Audrey Matlock designed this award-winning external dining room for financier Martin Harding near Sag Harbor, Long Island. Note the look-through fire area with suspended pulley shutter and state-of-the-art barbecue. Chairs are from French firm Triconfort and the table by Matlock.

BELOW In southern France a former barn was sensitively converted to provide modern comfort without expensive mod cons. Bugs proliferate in hot climes, so clean kitchens are vital: experts recommend using good old-fashioned bleach since newer antibacterial products have unlooked-for side-effects.

BELOW RIGHT Martin Harding's house is ideal for entertaining. He even keeps a box of cashmere blankets for guests for cooler evenings—true luxury. The structure provides shelter from extreme weather.

houses frequently employing staff), thus we too sampled the most delicious tagines of lamb in Marrakech, the best cuts of beef, barbecued, in America, and the freshest local fish, grilled, in South Africa. Food became a very important part of our journey through hot lands and something we greatly looked forward to on arrival, just like the Ottomans of old.

A unifying element of our culinary adventure was the lack of casual eating (meaning no TV dinners). Lunch was a relaxing and durable event, usually accompanied by rosé or other wine, just a little, and masses of water. It was, on the whole, served alfresco at noon (no later, to be able to squeeze in the ubiquitous siesta—not us, of course, since we had work to do) under arbors or sun shades, often by the pool or on the waterfront, and kept simple.

An added benefit to eating outdoors, and often cooking outside, too, is that kitchens and rooms for eating remain cleaner—bugs and bacteria thrive so in a warm arena, particularly a humid one—and terraces can simply be swept. Kitchens can be uncluttered and aesthetically pleasing, although they must use materials that are easy to keep clean. Wood, despite its porosity, is very clean, harboring fewer germs than plastic. It is also the most exquisite material to touch. Hence wood is a good choice for counters and chopping boards, particularly temperate hardwoods—oak, beech, and maple—which are strong and easy to maintain. Avoid tropical hardwoods in kitchens: they can be toxic if splintered.

TOP LEFT A myriad of woods create an extremely sophisticated space. The chameleon-like kitchen blends into the altogether seamless house (this is my kind of kitchen—truly, deeply chic). Breakfast stools and bar offer a view, too.

BOTTOM LEFT Fabric, fashion and interior designer Muriel Brandolini and husband Nuno bought their Hampton Bays waterfront spread a couple of years ago and made a jewel out of it, using her signature bright colors. The linear kitchen is open plan to the main living room.

ABOVE Mesh bar stools by Harry Bertoia nestle under a stone overhang in an essentially wood kitchen. When buying a new wood kitchen, look for environmentally responsible companies and wood from sustainable sources.

RIGHT, ABOVE Oh the luxury of space. I live in a London townhouse, my dining room doubling as office. Here is the dream of two dining tables, one formal, the other less so, just a few yards apart.

RIGHT Chairs in the right fabric provide comfort when dining inside. Since living in a hot climate often means a multitude of hard surfaces, fabric and upholstery are welcome, and help sound absorption.

FAR RIGHT In the South African beachside home, pickled wood cabinetry, handle-less with good pop-out action, has been made specifically for the house. The lengthy table is for dining and acts as a boundary between the kitchen area and the rest of the voluminous first floor.

FAR LEFT Hand-cut tiles are omnipresent in North Africa and the Middle East. Despite their strength and water-resistance, tiles are better for backsplashes than counters, unless you use epoxy grout or re-grout regularly, since grouting is easily stained. Vitrified tiles can work in any position.

LEFT Do not be fooled into thinking this is a bathroom. The tin sink is extremely deep and used for all manner of preparation in this African *rondavel* kitchen. Sinks should be shallow for comfort, but who can resist this beauty?

ABOVE & RIGHT To one end of a Provençal home, an almost medieval niche has been carved out of the house for relaxed evenings grilling. This is a true outdoor country kitchen, and even contains a rustic kind of counter, where meat and veggies are prepped. Logs are for use on the barbecue, which also adds warmth on cooler evenings. The only storage needed is for the timber, since plates and glasses are brought from the kitchen . Note the chic extractor hood.

OPPOSITE The colors of the outdoor chairs echo those inside, although the struts are in differing directions and the chair shape not the same—distant cousins. In a warm climate, the edges between indoor and out blur, and eating is often alfresco or at least at the cusp of the house boundaries. Here a link is made between the two via the furniture. A rustic setting can be effectively modernized with contemporary furniture and just a touch of accent color.

living

NATURAL FABRICS AND GRASSES, PLUS AN UNDERSTANDING OF AIR CURRENT, HAVE TO BE THE KEY TO COMFORTABLE HOT LIVING, WHETHER INSIDE OR OUT.

Sitting room, living room, drawing room, family: what is it to be? The main "living" room of the house is given different names depending upon various factors that include physical location (country), the grandness of the house and occupiers' social background. It may be the room in which the family congregates to watch television or entertain guests, but the term does not, to me, seem appropriate as the generic, since it sounds too casual, too informal. Drawing room is simply too grand a description for the way most of us live (the term has its roots in the "withdrawing" capacity—from the days when the parlor existed) and sitting room implies not much else happens in the room but waiting—a kind of antechamber to living. So I will stick with living room since it conjures some kind of activity, even if it is just the lounging variety.

Living in a hot climate does mean adopting a slower pace at least some of the time, and time management has to come into play. Just as we water plants at dawn or dusk, we should also enjoy heightened activity at these periods of the day (an early swim or run, perhaps tennis) since by midday the sun will encourage little more than a hearty lunch and afternoon nap. Working in a hot climate is another matter, although time management remains the key to success; a home office should be in the coolest part of the house, or where the temperature is most constant (see Karim El Achak's subterranean room or Johann Slee's artist studio), and the working day should be split into two definite portions, spanning more hours on the whole, but with a longer break in between.

The devices for keeping cool, whether at work or at play, remain the same, and great comfort can be achieved by the use of ceiling fans or understanding of air current. As a Londoner by birth and

LEFT In the main living quarter of a house built by Studio KO, windows are small so sunlight does not heat up the room by day. Furnishings, however, are warm, since evenings are cool in wintertime. The ottomans and rugs are local wares.

ABOVE This bookshelf in the east-facing study mimics the wrap form of the Melbourne house by BKK Architects. Although there is little place for clutter in a hot home, books are always welcome for stimulus and relaxation.

ABOVE With no central heating, fireplaces are integral to heating systems (unlike, ironically, in temperate climes, where they are often simply focal points). Karim El Achak's home delightfully blends Moroccan tradition and modernity.

currently by location, I am constantly amazed at how useless the Brits are at understanding convection and its relevance to traditional sash windows. These were invented so that you open the top by half and at the same time the bottom by half, so hot air escapes and cold air enters—so simple. Perhaps we have so few very warm days in the UK that the matter has not been dwelled upon—but in essence the instruction is clear: in any climate, get to know the physical capabilities of your architecture and use the spaces as they have been designed, since very little in architecture happens by accident. If you have louvers or shutters, experiment with them to achieve the coolest effect. Keep an eye on sun shades or scrim at windows, and be aware of the damaging effect of the sun on furniture and fabrics (installing mechanical sun shades that rise and fall automatically has never, to my mind, been successful since on days with some clouds and intermittent sun, the shades "go up and down like a whore's knickers," to quote photographer Ken Hayden).

Fabric plays an enormous role in keeping cool in a warm climate, and again it is science that helps us. Sheep keep cool in summer and warm in winter, and true wool (the coat of the domestic sheep as opposed to the wool of goats—angora or cashmere) is a very good material for climates where seasons swing from one extreme to another, although it should be used wisely and does not adapt to every furniture possibility—cottons and linens are better coverings for chairs than wool in a warm climate. One of the reasons wool works well in both climatic extremes is its insulating quality, due to the pockets of air it holds in its natural state and retains when woven.

OPPOSITE, TOP A pair of vast, beautiful wooden hinged doors open in two swift moves in this Auckland home. Simple, well-defined furniture helps any home. Floor-to-ceiling louvered glass panels bring ventilation and some light.

OPPOITE, BOTTOM Mysterious dark walls are traditional for an African enclosure. Although rooted in history, many features, such as the built-in seating, appear contemporary. With little space, the only option is to run seating around the perimeter.

ABOVE Cabinets in African mahogany flank the door to a house by Collett-Zarzycki, hiding a bar and hi-fi. Neutral natural fabrics and animal hides give cool comfort (whereas leather can feel sticky); in low humidity, staining on fabrics is not an issue.

RIGHT In an art collector's home on Long Island, he and Annabel Selldorf curated a collection of mid-20th-century furniture befitting the house's 1960s origins. The graphic fabric of the settle brings an element of masculinity.

Silk can also be used successfully in a warm climate, but can be less durable and less equipped for moisture, so is wiser left alone or used for throws. The best fibers for comfort and durability are cotton, as a fabric and as batting and padding, and linen. Cotton, incidentally, was first woven in pre-Inca Peru in around 200 BC, although the plant and fiber probably have origins in the Middle East since the word is derived from the Arabic *qutun*. Although now adapted to temperate growing zones, cotton, a species of spermatophyte (meaning seed-bearing), is a tropical plant and thrives best in high temperatures with a great deal of sunshine and abundant moisture. Like local woods that behave well in their own environments, cotton is durable and sturdy in moist, hot climates.

Linen is a luxury anywhere (it can be pricey) and particularly good in a hot climate—it remains cooler than the room temperature. It is good to wear, to lie in, and to sit upon; enjoy the creases, do not try to fight them. Linseed-filled bags are useful cooling devices when placed on a forehead, in cases of over-heating or a post-luncheon hangover. Linen fabric has many advantages over cotton because of its structure. It has a less "wooly" surface and does not soil as readily nor, being less spongy, does it absorb and retain moisture as easily. It is grown in temperate and cool climates and in wintertime in the subtropics. A woody fiber obtained from the flax stem, linen is slightly heavier than cotton but has twice its strength. Visually, it sits well with slate, wood, and stone, and is ideal for a rough-hewn, natural but elegant home.

LEFT Although a building merging with its landscape is a well-acknowledged idea for architects, when John Wardle created award-winning Balnarring Beach House, he decided not to draw the house into the landscape, but to seek a balance by separating the two, "developing opportunities to extend and frame views." The house and garden, according to the architect, do not inhabit the same space.

ABOVE American Poet William Carlos Williams (1883–1963) penned, "Is it any better in Heaven, my friend Ford, Than you found it in Provence?" ("To Ford Madox Ford in Heaven"). There is something magical about Provençal light that conjures outdoor living. The perfect combination of azure-blue sky, home-grown materials, and the scent of Provence— potent lavender and musty olive—just makes you want to sit outside!

RIGHT Just beyond the rear of the house built by Karim El Achak in the Moroccan city of Marrkech, a pergola shades alfresco life. Exterior living rooms have to be well shaded in the heat of the sun. Here, white muslin covers reflect the sun and remain cool to touch. Clara Candido, El Achak's Italian wife, has an import-export business, and many of the fabrics and objects are pieces she has collated.

bed

A GOOD BED IS FUNDAMENTAL TO LIFE ITSELF, AND SLEEP THE ONLY TRUE PANACEA TO PROBLEMS. UNADORNED BEDROOMS ARE SURELY THE MOST TRANQUIL, SO KEEP THEM SIMPLE AND PURE.

Sleeping alone in the heat is quite different from sleeping with someone, so ensure your bed is big enough to let you choose when to embrace and when to lie listless in solitude. Metaphysical poet John Donne had the right idea in "The Sun Rising": "This bed thy centre is, these walls thy sphere."

If the house works and the heat has been controlled by methods described earlier, the bedroom should be cool enough for slumber, although in some climates, particularly humid ones, even cooling does not mean total comfort. The best approach is to keep things simple and use empty space well: place the bed in the centre of the room so there is plenty of air circulating. Ensure it is raised from the ground with space underneath (box bed bases might be good for storage but increase heat and dust). Floors should be comfortable under bare feet, but rugs and carpets will often feel too hot or fusty.

ABOVE Floor-to-ceiling glazing gives light and a view. Blind mechanisms are hidden between ceiling and glazing, which cascades past floor level. The chair is re-edition Swan by Arne Jacobsen (designed 1957–8).

RIGHT A leather-upholstered inverted T frame supports a bed and, beyond the "wall," a sofa. This is the bedroom equivalent of a stylish kitchen's central workstation, and works well in a warm climate.

RIGHT, ABOVE If you live in a region popular with guests, a bedroom chair can be a solace from the world. A good read and a view is all you need. In John Wardle's Balnarring house, sliding doors open gracefully to nature.

Pillows for head support should be kept to a minimum, and fashion pillows should be avoided (no matter what the climate, there is rarely a place for a spare cushion).

Sheets should be cotton or linen, and simple, in plain whites or neutrals, and bedclothes should not touch the floors as they will gather dust. Layering is key to comfortable sleeping, just as for clothing: different weights added one on top of another when temperatures drop. There is something reassuring about a little swaddling, and with cotton and linen you can lie wrapped and still keep cool. Linen is cool to the touch, and hence unparalleled in intense heat. Duvets are rarely needed in warm climates.

Many of the houses we visited incorporated large windows in bedrooms for the view. Witnessing the great outdoors from within can help reduce the feeling of claustrophobia in high temperatures. Better

still, if you can, attach a little outside space to the bedroom by way of a balcony or terrace, also lovely for early-morning breakfasts in peace (if you have guests, then the fluster of hospitality can also make life more uncomfortable in a hot climate, so take it easy, pace yourself).

Some architects even switch the plan of a house to make sure the bedroom has features usually reserved for living spaces. Johann and Rene Slee's bedroom leads straight to the pool at the front of their South African house. Again in South Africa, Silvio Rech and Lesley Carstens leap from their bed into living since their bedroom, both logistically and emotionally, is the heartbeat of their home.

Storage is a necessity but the less movement the better in a warm house, so keep clothes folded neatly at waist height and hanging items easy to reach. A wardrobe, like a home, should always be edited to necessities—there is no place for surplus in the modern, contained world.

LEFT This South African room is very basic indeed, its built-in shelf and wall recess the only adornment. If it were not palatial, it would appear almost cell-like! But is this not the way to live with all action outside?

ABOVE A bedroom requires just the basics, four walls and a bed, as long as there is room for storing clothes and a good bathroom nearby, preferably connected. This exposed-brick room is rural French.

BELOW LEFT A child's room can be clutter-free, but should be a happy place. In Hampton Bays, New York, Muriel Brandolini has painted pretty horizontal stripes and created flora-inspired headboards.

BELOW As seen in this art dealer's home in the Hamptons, New York, I tend to prefer a high bed, the best crisp sheets, plump pillows, and a jolly good mattress: a no-nonsense approach, almost hospital chic.

ABOVE Small spaces make sense in a second home, or where outdoors takes precedence. A rather neat structure houses all the necessary trappings for sleep and study away from home in this teenager's room.

RIGHT Decoration can be too visually stimulating, but smart, bold paint strokes add panache. In Marrakech, Karim El Achak and his wife's bedroom exhibits extreme tidiness yet robust character.

TOP, LEFT TO RIGHT The freestanding tub (here beside a low floating wall) is the original bathing system: the bath used to be a tub filled by hand. This is a modern version, unadorned and floating. Duravit makes very good systems.

A tailormade sunken concrete bathtub for two, side-by-side, plus shower, in a scheme by Seth Stein. Sunken tubs usually look good and may leave more space for a window. They are, however, quite difficult to negotiate, so beware.

This is a fantastic corridor of a bathroom where the tub simply fits between an exterior deck and the interior. Sliding panes offer protection if required. The enclosure has strong lines and a gorgeous blend of materials.

I prefer bathrooms that echo Greece and Rome. Here the proportions and mosaic tiles give a nod to the ancients, while modernity brings good lighting and an unlimited supply of water. The ladder is cleverly placed to hold towels.

BOTTOM, LEFT TO RIGHT Even a tiny bathroom can sport an ample period bathtub. Visual comfort is more important than physical comfort in a bathroom, as long as the bath is right. This mellow mix of warm woods is modern African serenity.

Mosaics are a traditional addition to a bathroom and these days usually appear in one color for simplicity. Italian firm Bisazza produces the best mosaic pieces today; hand- or machine-made, they arrive in a palette for easy assembly.

This custom-design is a first for my eyes: a double-length tub for two to sit opposite each other. A lovely idea, but large baths use masses of water, unlike showers; think of the environment and ensure there are two of you in a bath this big.

A bathroom mirror provides time for reflection, both visually and contemplatively, pure white surroundings emptying the mind as the shower cleanses the body. This circular mirror has its fellow by shape in the circular shower rod.

bath

HAPPY LIVING IS LIVING FREE, PERHAPS NOWHERE MORE THAN IN THE BATHROOM—ESPECIALLY IN HOT LANDS, WHERE WE CRAVE TO WASH AWAY SWEAT AND TROUBLE, EMERGING COOL AND COMFORTABLE.

"Good God! To have a room of one's own with a real fire and books and tea and company, and no dinner bells and distractions, and a little time for doing something! It is a wonderful vision, and surely worth some risks."

At first glance you may think this manifesto, which became emblematic of the loose circle of friends known as the Bloomsbury Group in early-20th-century London, is an extract from Virginia Woolf's now famous feminist tract of 1926, *A Room of One's Own*, in which she describes women's oppression in terms of denied space. It is, in fact, the words of Lytton Strachey in a 1909 missive to Duncan Grant, which expresses the longing of the two homosexual men to escape the conventions of bourgeois domesticity they found just as stifling as did their female counterparts. *A Room of One's Own* eventually became a symbol for the struggle to create a more enabling form of domesticity associated with modern life. It was unpredictably the shared emphasis on domesticity that bound the women and men of Bloomsbury into a community more cohesive than more avant-garde groupings of the time.

To feel stifled in any sense is abhorrent, and in the modern world there should be no need for isolation, unless chosen, nor pressure, which is rarely chosen, and I suppose if there is a room that has

adapted to suit the way we live today it is the bathroom. It is a room of one's own where all manner of problems—psychological, physical, and emotional—can be flushed away.

Bathrooms today are spacious, simple, fully functioning, and convenient. They are for relaxation and reclining, as well as activity. Successful bathing, in any weather, is effortless bathing, and you know you are really free from restraint when you don't even have a door to the washing facility, or if it is actually outdoors.

Choosing to live in the wilderness or in a manner considered radical, which is perhaps just the way you want to be, is a freedom we should all be granted. The only pressure we should feel is from the best-available shower hose as we wash away the daily grime and all that goes with it.

Less than a century ago, being free for Vanessa Bell and Virginia Woolf meant "we should all leave Kensington and start afresh in Bloomsbury," which seems far from radical,

almost quaint. In reality, the few miles involved meant a new life, as Bell stated: "All that seemed to matter was that at last we were free, had rooms of our own and space in which to be alone." Later she wrote, "It seemed that in every way we were making a new beginning in the tall clean rather frigid rooms."

Deciding to live in a hot climate, far from the madding crowd, to seek one's own life (many who do seek a hot climate have made a conscious decision to opt out of their normal, more restrictive lifestyles, whether it be for retirement or just a new start), is a brave move not without manifold challenges. In a way, if you do seek the sun, you are paving the way for others to follow, since you will be developing better ways to cope with its effects in a world whose climate is changing rapidly. Sun-seekers tend to be pioneers like the Bloomsbury Group in one way, and in another merely desirous of "books and tea and company"—sometimes in the bathroom!

ABOVE LEFT A central workstation for bathing. KO architects divided this Moroccan bedroom with a suspended double wall containing narrow closets. The vanity unit with double sink is "hung" on the wall.

ABOVE TOP As free-standing tubs are back, so are basins placed on furniture. Boffi produces fine basins and bathroom accessories in glass, stone, and porcelain.

ABOVE In Karim El Achak's Moroccan "granny annex," hand-cut tiles vary in color and patina, creating a traditional image.

BELOW Contrasting tiles denote different functions. This is a wet room in that the shower is uncontained, but the glass door prevents spillage. Wet rooms are making more of an appearance (RainSky by Dornbracht is the ultimate: water seems to fall from the ceiling).

RIGHT An innovative homegrown affair, this shower falls from a wrought-iron curlew frame in an outdoor niche enclosed by doors to the bathroom (seen here) and bedroom, plus garden foliage.

BOTTOM LEFT A train of shower cubicles plus toilet serves four children (see pages 27–9). It is spruced up by the random patterning of varnished concrete.

BOTTOM CENTER I want to alert design aficionados to "liquid space," a phrase newly arrived in design vocabulary. It was coined by architecture and design critic Stefano Casciani, of Domus. Fluid is how we now perceive and define space.

BOTTOM RIGHT Carved into the Johannesburg house, this wet room has an uneven floor so water drains without flooding. The tall slit window and its frame open fully to the forest beyond.

DIRECTORY

APPLIANCES

Asko
PO Box 851805, Richardson, TX 75085, USA
Tel: +1 (972) 644-8595
www.askousa.com
Eco-friendly household appliances.

In-Sink-Erator
4700 21st Street, Racine, WI 53406, USA
Tel: +1 (800) 656-9226
www.insinkerator.com
Eco-friendly waste-disposal/household appliances.

Thermador
5551 McFadden Avenue, Huntington Beach, CA 92649, USA
www.thermador.com
Advanced kitchen and refrigeration systems.

ARCHITECTS

Paolo Badesco
Viale di Porta Vercellina 5, 20123 Milano, Italy
Tel: +39 (0)24-100737
Fax: +39 (0)24-982309
www.paolobadesco.it
paolobadesco@libero.it

BKK Architects
Level 9, 180 Russell Street, Melbourne 3000, Victoria, Australia
Tel: +61 (0)3-9671-4555
Fax: +61 (0)3-9671-4666
www.b-k-k.com.au

Muriel Brandolini
New York
www.murielbrandolini.com

Patrick Clifford
Architectus, 1 Centre Street, PO Box 90621, AMSC, Freemans Bay, Auckland, New Zealand
Tel: +64 (0)9-307-5970
Fax: +64 (0)9-307-5972
www.architectus.com.au

Collett-Zarzycki Architects & Designers
Fernhead Studios, 2b Fernhead Road, London W9 3ET, UK
Tel: +44 (0)20-8969-6967
www.collett-zarzycki.com

Steven Ehrlich
10865 Washington Boulevard, Culver City, CA 90232, USA
Tel: +1 (310) 838-9700
Fax: +1 (310) 838-9737
www.s-ehrlich.com

Karim El Achak Architect
7 rue de la Liberté, Marrakech, Morroco
Tel: +212 44 44 73 13
associati@menara.ma

Ramon Esteve
Estudio de Arquitectura, Jorge Juan 8, 5º, 11ª – 46004 Valencia, Spain
Tel. +34 (9)6-351-04-34
www.ramonesteve.com

Karl Fournier and Olivier Martin
Studio K O, Paris and Marrakech
Tel: +33 (0)1-42-71-1392
komarrakech@studioko.fr
koparis@studioko.fr

Virginie Gravière, Olivier Martin
139 rue Belleville, 330000 Bordeaux, France
Tel/fax: +33 (0)5-56-98-2381
martin.graviere@wanadoo.fr

Lautner Associates
8055 W. Manchester Ave, Suite 705, Playa del Rey, CA 90293, USA
Tel: +1 (310) 577-7783
Fax: +1 (310) 577-7793
www.lautnerassociates.com

Steve Martino
3336 North 32nd Street, Phoenix, AR 85018, USA
Tel: +1 (602) 957-6150
www.stevemartino.net

Audrey Matlock Architects
88 West Broadway, New York, NY 10007, USA
Tel: +1 (212) 267-2378
Fax: +1 (212) 267-6850
www.audreymatlock.com

Ian Moore
EngelenMoore, 44 McLachlan Ave, Rushcutters Bay, Sydney 2011, NSW, Australia
Tel: +61 (0)2-9380-4099
Fax: +61 (0)2-9380-4302
www.engelenmoore.com.au

Clinton Murray Architects
2 King Street, Merimbula, NSW 2548, Australia
Tel +61 (0)2-6495-1964
www.clintonmurray.com.au

Silvio Rech/Lesley Carstens
Architecture & Interior Architecture
Tel: + 27 (0)829-009935
Fax: +27 (0)11-486-1525
adventarch@mweb.co.za

Annabel Selldorf
Selldorf Architects, 62 White Street, New York, NY 10013, USA.
Tel +1 (212) 219-9571
Fax: +1 (212) 941-6362
www.selldorf.com

Johann Slee
Slee Architects & Interiors, 32 Pallinghurst Rd, Westcliff 2193, South Africa;
PO Box 72182, ParkView 2122, Johannesburg, South Africa

Tel: +27 (0)11-646-9935
Fax: +27 (0)11-486-2045
johann@slee.co.za

Seth Stein Architects
15 Grand Union Centre, West Row, Ladbroke Grove, London W10 5AS, UK
Tel: +44 (0)20-8968-8581
www.sethstein.com

Bart Voorsanger
Voorsanger & Associates, Architects PC, 246 West 38th Street, New York, NY 10018, USA
Tel: +1 (212) 302-6464
Fax: +1 (212) 840-0063
info@voorsanger.com
www.voorsanger.com

John Wardle Architects
Level 10, 180 Russell Street, Melbourne 3000, Victoria, Australia
www.johnwardle.com

ARCHITECTURAL SALVAGE

Irreplaceable Artifacts
216 East 125th Street, New York, NY 10035-1738, USA
Tel: +1 (212) 860-1138
Fax: +1 (212) 860-1560
Or: 428 Main Street, Middletown, CT 06457, USA
Tel: +1 (860) 344-8576
Fax: +1 (860) 638-0834
www.irreplaceableartifacts.com

Materials Unlimited
2 West Michigan Avenue, Michigan, MI 48197, USA

Retrouvius
32 York House, Upper Montagu Street, London W1H 1FR, UK
Tel: +44 (0)20-7724-3387

AWNINGS & BLINDS

Luxaflex
UK
Tel: +44 (0)800-652-7799
www.luxaflex.com
Blinds and window treatments.

Thomas Sanderson
UK
Tel: +44 (0)800-220-603
www.thomassanderson.com
Conservatory blinds, patio awnings, and window shutters.

BAMBOO

American Bamboo Society
www.americanbamboo.org

Bamboo Society of Australia
www.bamboo.org.au

La Bambouseraie
www.bambouseraie.fr

Environmental Bamboo Foundation
www.bamboocentral.org

Wild Bamboo Organization
www.worldbamboo.org

CERAMICS & TILES

Bisazza
60 Sloane Avenue, London SW3 3DD, UK
Tel: +44 (0)20-7584-8837
Fax: +44 (0)20-7584-8838
www.bisazza.com
Glass mosaic tiles.

Ceramica Flaminia
SS Flaminia Km 54,630, 01033 Civita Castellana (VT), Italy
Tel: +39 (0)761-542030
www.ceramicaflaminia.it
Bathroom ceramics.

Ceramica Viva
www.cerviva.it
Ceramic tiles in contemporary styles.

ECO-ARCHITECTURE

Doerr
2227 Canyon Boulevard, Boulder, CO 80302, USA
Full-service architecture firm serving the Rocky Mountain region of the US.

FABRIC

Donghia
485 Broadway, New York, NY 10013, USA
Tel: +1 (212) 925-2777
www.donghia.com
Furniture, accessories, textiles.

Maharam
www.maharam.com
New York-based family-run firm: contemporary and re-edition classics.

FLOORING

Amtico International Inc.
200 Lexington Avenue, Suite 809, New York, NY 10016, USA
Tel: +1 (800) 291-885
Fax: +1 (212) 545-8382
www.amtico.com
Replicate stone, wood, slate, glass tiles.

Ann Sacks Tile & Stone
204 East 58th Street, New York, NY 10022, USA
Tel: +1 (800) 278-8453
www.annsacks.com
Glass metal-leafed tiles, ceramic tiles.

Armstrong
2500 Columbia Avenue, Lancaster, PA 17604, USA
Tel: +1 (800) 233-3823
www.armstrongfloors.com
Manufacturers of vinyl, laminates, and hardwood flooring.

Artistic Tile
79 5th Avenue, New York, NY 10003, USA
Tel: +1 (212) 727-9331
Glass and ceramic tiles.

Country Floors

15 East 16th Street, New York, NY 10003, USA
Tel: +1 (212) 627-8300
Ceramic and marble tiles.

Hastings Tile & Il Bagno
230 Park Avenue South, New York, NY 10003, USA
Tel: +1 (212) 674-9700
Glass tiles and bathroom fittings.

The Original Decking Company
www.originaldecking.co.uk
Garden decking/carpentry.

The Original Stone Company
100/105 Victoria Crescent, Burton on Trent DE14 2QF, UK
Tel: +44 (0)1283-501090
Natural stone flooring.

Pergo
PO Box 1775, Horsham, PA 19044, USA
Tel: +1 (800) 337-3746
www.pergo.com
Manufacturers of laminate flooring.

Slate World
Green World, 97 Tomiano Avenue, London NW5 2RX, UK
Tel: +44 (0)20-8204-3444
www.slateworld.com
Quality slate roofing and flooring tiles. Products include gray, green, black, red, and multicolor tiles from quarries around the world.

Stone Age
3 Parsons Green Lane, London SW6 4HH, UK
Tel: +44 (0)20-7384-9090
www.estone.co.uk
Specialist suppliers of natural stone flooring, contemporary stone floors, or limestone flooring.

UK Marble Ltd
21 Nurcott Road, Hereford HR4 9LW, UK
Wide range of marble.

Vanderhurd Studio
260 5th Avenue, Suite 11S, New York, NY 10001, USA
Tel: +1 (212) 343-9070
Modern carpets by Christine Van Der Hurd.

Vermont Structural Slate
PO Box 98, 3 Prospect Street, Fair Haven, VT 05743, USA
Tel: +1 (800) 343-1900
Fax: +1 (802) 265-3865
www.vermontstructuralslate.com
Specialist suppliers of slate.

Walker & Zanger
13190 Telfair Avenue, Sylmar, CA 91342, USA
Tel: +1 (713) 300-2940
www.walkerzanger.com
Natural stone and ceramic, metal, and glass tile.

FURNITURE

Bernhardt Design
1839 Morganton Blvd, PO Box 740, Lenoir, NC 28645, USA
Tel: +1 (828) 758-9811
European distribution: Natural Elements Ltd, 53-56 Great Sutton Street, Clerkenwell, London EC1V 0DG, UK
Tel: +44 (0)20-7253-2111
Fax: +44 (0)20-7253-0111
www.bernhardtdesign.com
Greenguard-certified contemporary furniture.

Dedon
Zeppelinstrasse 22, Lüneburg 21337, Germany
Tel: +49 (0)4131-22-44-70
Fax: +49 (0)4131-22-44-730
www.dedon.de
Outdoor furniture.

Gandia Blasco
www.gandiablasco.com
Garden, poolside, and interior furniture.

Habitat
Tel: +44 (0)845-601-0740
www.habitat.co.uk
Contemporary furniture for home and garden.

Lloyd Loom Furniture
3/13 Chelsea Harbour, London SW10 0XE, UK
Tel: +44 (0)20-7352-2312
www.vincentsheppard.com
Iconic wicker furniture.

Fritz Hansen
Allerodvej 8, Allerod   3450, Denmark
Tel: +45 (0)86-554415
www.fritzhansen.com
Manufacturer of Danish and Scandinavian design.

Pucci International
44 West 18th Street, 12 Floor, New York, NY 10011, USA
tel: +1 (212) 633-0452
www.ralph-pucci.com
Quality furniture by Andrée Putman, Chris Lehreche, re-edition Eileen Gray rugs; by appointment.

The Knoll Group
105 Wooster Street, New York, NY 10012, USA
Tel: +1 (212) 343-4180
www.knoll.com
Modern furniture designs by Marcel Breuer, Eero Saarinen, Mies Van Der Rohe, and Ettore Sottsass.

FURNITURE STORES

ABC Carpet & Home
881/888 Broadway, New York, NY 10003, USA
Tel: +1 (212) 473-3000
www.abchome.com
Tasteful collections of home furnishings and carpets from all over the world: environment-conscious.

B&B Italia
250 Brompton Road, London SW3 2AS,   UK
Tel: +44 (0)20-7591-8111
www.bebitalia.it
Quality contemporary furniture by Antonio Citterio, Patricia Urquiola, and others.

Moss
146 Greene Street, New York, NY 10012, USA
Tel: +1 (212) 226-2190
www.mossonline.com
New York emporium of up-to-the-minute furniture, glassware, flatware.

GLASS

AEC Portico
www.aecportico.co.uk
A link to the building and construction industry.

Contract Glass
www.contractglass.co.uk
Shelves, bar tops, sink tops, reception desks, bridges, glass floors.

Corning
www.corning.com
World's leading glass producers, specializing in a range of technology-led product sectors.

Omnidecor
Italy
www.omnidecor.it
An international group based in Erba (Como, Italy), a market leader in the manufacture of high-quality satined glass for interior design and architecture, from partitions to furniture components and façades for entire buildings.

Saint Gobain
www.saint-gobain-glass.com
International glass firm with many divisions, also producing "low-E" glass.

INTERIOR DESIGN

Martin Brudnizki Design Studio
2L Chelsea Reach,79/89 Lots Road,   London SW10 0RN, UK
Tel: +44 (0)20-7376-7555
Fax: +44 (0)20-7376-7444
www.mbds.net
Interior Architect with projects in Europe, South America, and Asia.

Terry Hunziker Inc.
208 3rd Avenue South, Seattle, WA 98104, USA
Tel: +1 (206) 467-1144
Fax: +1 (206) 467-7061
Seattle-based interior design and architecture.

KITCHENS & BATHROOMS

Alessi
155 Spring Street, New York, NY 10012, USA
Tel: +1 (212) 431-1310
www.alessi.com
Accessories for kitchen and home.

Bulthaup
www.bulthaup.com
Quality kitchen design with holistic approach.

Bed, Bath & Beyond
650 Liberty Avenue, Union, NJ, USA
Tel: +1 (800) 0462-3966
www.bedbath.com
Retailer of home accessories.

Bizhan LLC
40 East 19th Street, New York, NY 10003 , USA
Tel: +1 (212) 982-6969
Fax: +1 (212) 982-6868
www.bizhan.com
Contemporary furniture solutions.

Boffi
3112 Green Street, New York, NY 10013, USA
Tel: +1 (212) 431-8282
www.boffisoho.com
The Aston Martin of bathrooms and kitchens, designed by Piero Lissoni, Luigi Maaoni, and Norbert Wangen; also Marcel Wanders pipe shower. A must for the discerning.

Crate & Barrel
1860 Jefferson Avenue, Naperville, IL 60540, USA
Tel:+1 (800) 967-6696
www.crateandbarrel.com
Useful and simple objects and furniture for the home, well priced.

Grohe
www.grohe.com
Faucets and kitchen and bathroom accessories. Largest exporter of taps worldwide.

Home Depot
2455 Pace Ferry Road, Atlanta, GA 30339, USA
Tel: +1 (800) 553-3199
www.homedepot.com
Online source for home building and decoration, listing 30,000 companies.

Sur La Table
www.surlatable.com
1765 6th Avenue South, Seattle, WA 98134, USA
Tel: +1 (800) 243-0852
Online source for everything to do with cooking and eating.

Waterworks
469 Broome Street, New York, NY 10013, USA
Tel: +1 (212) 966-0605
Fax: +1 (212) 966-6747
www.waterworks.com
Lifestyle retailer for bath and kitchen.

Williams Sonoma Inc.
3250 Van Ness Avenue, San Francisco, CA 94109, USA
Tel: +1 (800) 840-2592
www.williams-sonomainc.com
Stylish American pots and pans, linens, small items for the home, home accessories (good bridal registry).

LIGHTING

Artemide
46 Greene Street,   New York, NY 10012, USA
Tel: +1 (212) 925-1588
www.artemide.com
Lamps and lights, indoor, outdoor, and architectural.

Flos
www.flos.com
Italian-based international lighting firm still selling designs by Achille Castiglioni, whom they discovered, as well as others, including lights by Philippe Starck.

PAINT

Benjamin Moore & Co
51 Chestnut Ridge Road, Montvale, NJ 07645, USA
Tel: +1 (201) 573-9600, +1 (800) 344-0400
www.benjaminmoore.com

SURFACES

Abet Laminates
60 West Sheffield Avenue, Englewood, NJ 07631, USA
Tel: +1 (201) 541-0701
Surface laminates in colors and neutrals.

Du Pont Corian
Barley Mill Plaza, PO BOX 80012, Wilmington, DE 19880, USA
Tel: +1 (800) 436-7426
www.corian.com
Producers of Corian ® hard surfaces, for interior and architectural use.

SWIMMING POOLS

Aqualift
France
Tel: +33 (0)6-17-73-6163
www.aqualift.fr
Suppliers of technology swimming pools that disappear to become hard surface when not in use (the bottom rises).

Award Pools & Landscapes
PO BOX 6763, Bauklan Hills Business Centre, NSW 2153, Australia
Tel: +61 (0)2-9629-3639
www.awardpools.com.au
Garden and landscape.

Endless Pools
200 Dutton Mill Road, Aston, PA 19014, USA
www.endlesspools.co.uk
Endless-pool components fit through standard doorways, so installation is possible in existing interiors (basements/garages).

Freedom Pools
417 Manns Road, West Gosford, NSW 2250, Australia
Tel: +61 (0)2-4325-0813
Fax: +61 (0)2-4325-0821
www.freedompools.com.au
The Australian Central Coast's swimming-pool-construction experts.

Imagination Design Concepts
588 Perugia Road, Los Angeles, CA 90077, USA
Tel: +1 (310) 471-5024
thornbury@earthlink.net
Garden and landscape design tackling a wide range of architecturally led projects.

Natural Designs
3750 West Indian School Road, Phoenix, AR 85019, USA
Tel: +1 (602) 532-3700
www.shastapools.com
Specializing in building pools in arid climates; based in Arizona.

Patrick Mazure
Tel: +33 (0)4-74-08-1621
www.piscines-mazure.com
Swimming-pool design using glass.

Peter Glass and Associates
2/69 Christie Street, St Leonards, NSW 2065, Australia
Tel: +61 (0)2-9906-2727
www.peterglass.com.au
Landscape architects, environmental planners, pool designers.

Pool Design
UK
Tel: +44 (0)1666-840065
www.pool-design.co.uk
Designers of pools, many incorporated into listed buildings. Good with planning applications.

Yves Zoccola
Les Bonfillions, Satin-Marc-Jaumergarde 13100, France
Tel: +33 (0)4-42-24-9343
www.decopiscine.com
Self-confessed "water sculptor", designing pools mainly in France.

INDEX

Figures in italics indicate captions.

picture credits

All photographs by Andrew Wood unless stated otherwise.

Every effort has been made to trace the copyright holders, architects and designers and we apologise in advance for any unintentional omission and would be pleased to insert the appropriate acknowledgement in any subsequent edition

1 Paolo Badesco's villa in Italy; 2 Johann Slee's home in Johannesburg; 4-5 a house in Ibiza, designed by Ramón Esteve Architects; 6-7 Richard & Lucille Lewin's House In Plettenberg Bay South Africa, designed by Seth Stein; 9 above Richard & Lucille Lewin's House In Plettenberg Bay South Africa, designed by Seth Stein; 9 below a house in Ibiza, designed by Ramón Esteve Architects; 10 above left a house in Marrakech, designed by Karl Fournier and Olivier Marty, Studio KO; 10 above centre Johann Slee's home in Johannesburg; 10 above right a house in Ibiza, designed by Ramón Esteve Architects; 10 centre left a house near Grasse, France, designed by Collett-Zarzycki Architects & Designers; 10 centre Richard & Lucille Lewin's House In Plettenberg Bay South Africa, designed by Seth Stein; 10 centre right a house in Marrakech, designed by Karl Fournier and Olivier Marty, Studio KO; 10 below left a house in Victoria, Australia, designed by Black Kosloff Knott; 10 below centre a house in Balnarring in coastal Victoria, designed by John Wardle Architects; 10 below right a house in Ibiza, designed by Ramón Esteve Architects; 11 a house in Victoria, Australia, designed by Clinton Murray; 12 a house in New South Wales designed by Clinton Murray; 13 a house near Grasse, France, designed by Collett-Zarzycki Architects & Designers; 19-25 a house in Tucson, Arizona, garden, pool and courtyard designed by Steve Martino, FASLA, interior design by Voorsanger & Associates; 26-29 a house in Marrakech, designed by Karl Fournier and Olivier Marty, Studio KO; 30-33 a house in North Province, South Africa, designed by Collett-Zarzycki Architects & Designers; 34-38 Patrick Clifford's house in Auckland designed by Architectus; 40-43 Johann Slee's home in Johannesburg; 44-47 Silvio Rech & Lesley Carstens' house near Johannesburg; 49 a house in Johannesburg, designed by Johann Slee; 50-53 a house near Grasse, France, designed by Collett-Zarzycki Architects & Designers; 54-59 Karim El Achak's house in Marrakech; 60-63 a house in Italy designed by Paolo Badesco; 65-69 a house in Bordeaux, designed by Virginie Gravière & Olivier Martin; 70-73 Richard & Lucille Lewin's House In Plettenberg Bay South Africa, designed by Seth Stein; 74-77 a house in New South Wales designed by Clinton Murray; 79-84 John and Marilyn Roscoe's house in California, designed by Helena Arahuete Architect of Lautner Associates; 86-91 a house in Ibiza, designed by Ramón Esteve Architects; 92-95 a house near Cape Town designed by Johann Slee; 97-101 a house in Victoria, Australia, designed by Black Kosloff Knott; 102-107 Steven Ehrlich, FAIA's house in Venice, California; 108-111 John & Susan Wardle's house in Melbourne, designed by John Wardle Architects; 112-113 a house in Johannesburg, designed by Johann Slee; 117 a house in New South Wales designed by Clinton Murray; 118 a house near Grasse, France, designed by Collett-Zarzycki Architects & Designers; 119 above left a house

in Italy designed by Paolo Badesco; 119 above right a house in Bordeaux, designed by Virginie Gravière & Olivier Martin; 119 below left Steven Ehrlich, FAIA's house in Venice, California; 119 below centre a house in Tuscon, Arizona, garden designed by Steve Martino, interior design by Voorsanger & Associates; 119 below right Graham Head (of ABC Carpet & Home) and Barbara Rathborne's house in Long Island; 120 above left Patrick Clifford's house in Auckland designed by Architectus; 120 above centre Patrick Clifford's house in Auckland designed by Architectus; 120 above right John & Susan Wardle's house in Melbourne, designed by John Wardle Architects; 120 below left John and Marilyn Roscoe's house in California, designed by Helena Arahuete Architect of Lautner Associates; 120 below right a house in Balnarring in coastal Victoria, designed by John Wardle Architects; 121 a house in Tuscon, Arizona, garden designed by Steve Martino, interior design by Voorsanger & Associates; 122 left a house near Cape Town designed by Johann Slee; 122 right a house in Tuscon, Arizona, garden designed by Steve Martino, interior design by Voorsanger & Associates; 123 a house in Johannesburg, designed by Johann Slee; 124 above left John and Marilyn Roscoe's house in California, designed by Helena Arahuete Architect of Lautner Associates; 124 above centre a house near Grasse, France, designed by Collett-Zarzycki Architects & Designers; 124 above right a house near Cape Town designed by Johann Slee; 124 below a house near Grasse, France, designed by Collett-Zarzycki Architects & Designers; 125 a house in Tuscon, Arizona, garden designed by Steve Martino, interior design by Voorsanger & Associates; 126 a house in Italy designed by Paolo Badesco; 127 above left Steven Ehrlich, FAIA's house in Venice, California; 127 above centre Karim El Achak's house in Marrakech; 127 above right a house in Tuscon, Arizona, garden designed by Steve Martino, interior design by Voorsanger & Associates; 127 below Johann Slee's home in Johannesburg; 128 left Silvio Rech & Lesley Carstens' house near Johannesburg; 128 right a house in Marrakech, designed by Karl Fournier and Olivier Marty, Studio KO; 129 a house in Marrakech, designed by Karl Fournier and Olivier Marty, Studio KO; 130 Johann Slee's home in Johannesburg; 131 above left a house in Bordeaux, designed by Virginie Gravière & Olivier Martin; 131 above centre Steven Ehrlich, FAIA's house in Venice, California; 131 above right Patrick Clifford's house in Auckland designed by Architectus; 131 below a house in Marrakech, designed by Karl Fournier and Olivier Marty, Studio KO; 132 John and Marilyn Roscoe's house in California, designed by Helena Arahuete Architect of Lautner Associates; 133 left Steven Ehrlich, FAIA's house in Venice, California; 133 above right a house in Tucson, Arizona, garden, pool and courtyard designed by Steve Martino, FASLA, interior design by Voorsanger & Associates; 133 below right Steven Ehrlich, FAIA's house in Venice, California; 134 left Karim El Achak's house in Marrakech; 134 right Patrick Clifford's house in Auckland designed by Architectus; 134-135 Johann Slee's home in Johannesburg; 136 John and Marilyn Roscoe's house in California, designed by Helena Arahuete Architect of Lautner Associates; 137 left a house in Bordeaux, designed by Virginie Gravière & Olivier Martin; 137 centre Richard & Lucille Lewin's House In Plettenberg Bay South Africa, designed by Seth Stein; 137 right a house in Bordeaux, designed by Virginie Gravière & Olivier Martin; 138 left Johann Slee's home in Johannesburg; 138 centre Paolo Badesco's villa in Italy; 138 right a house in Bordeaux, designed by Virginie Gravière & Olivier Martin; 139 a

acknowledgements

The author would like to thank all those who collaborated on the book, the architects, designers and home owners, those nature lovers who had the foresight to be committed to sustainable building, but particularly Martin Harding, Johann and Rene Slee, Andrzej Zarzycki and family, Barbara Rathborne and Graham Head, and Lucille and Richard Lewin for their boundless hospitality. Thanks are also due to my ever-patient and burgeoning family, to Paul and the boys, and to Jacqui, Kate, Lawrence, and Cathy, the team.